Grossed-Out Surgeon Vomits Inside Patient!

Grossed-Out Surgeon Vomits Inside Patient!

An Insider's Look at Supermarket Tabloids

Jim Hogshire

FERAL HOUSE

Grossed-Out Surgeon Vomits Inside Patient! © 1997 by Jim Hogshire

Edited by Alexandra Behr
Interior design by Margaret Murray

9 8 7 6 5 4 3 2 1

For a free catalogue of publications, send SASE to:
Feral House • 2532 Lincoln Blvd. • Suite 359 • Venice, CA 90291

Table of Contents

♦ ♦ ♦

Introduction

Tabloid Exposé—Spiked by *The Nation*

In the spring of 1991 I proposed an article to *The Nation* that would give a behind-the-scenes look at the tabloids based on my experiences as a staff writer and stringer for nearly all the supermarket tabs.

I had planned to use the Palm Beach rape case involving William Kennedy Smith as a springboard to examine the tabloids' influence on mainstream media and society. The connection seemed obvious: By naming the alleged victim, the tabloids generated the controversy and were shaping the tone of the mainstream press' trial coverage.

The *New York Times,* NBC and other mainstream media criticized each other for releasing "sensational stories" of the alleged victim's lurid past. Like NBC, the *Times* had named the victim. The matter had become a moral problem that needed explanation. Surely this sleazy behavior mimicked tabloids' shameless exploitation techniques. The media elite decried mainstream press' shabby actions and placed the blame on "tabloid journalism." Any story to support this theory was welcomed.

An insider's perspective like mine could illuminate how such upstanding journalists had become so perverted. To do that I would reveal neat little secrets about the shameful rags, which the editors at *The Nation* were eager to snap up. Please write it, they asked me, and quickly.

Nation bigshot Micah Sifrey called me to say she assigned editor Dick Pollack. Dick gave me his private number at a vacation get-away, so I'd be sure to stay in touch. Depending on how juicy my information was, he told me, they may just want to "scramble" the story for the next issue.

I worked feverishly on it and faxed the story to Dick. No reply. Days passed, the issue appeared and nobody had "scrambled" my important story. When I got through to Dick, he said the story was an utter failure. He not only vehemently disagreed that supermarket tabloids had any influence on mainstream media, but said that even if they did, my article gave no proof.

Sifrey had another complaint: Wasn't this supposed to be an exposé of the tabloids' sleazy and unjournalistic ways? In his opinion I hadn't exposed them at all. I had made the supermarket tabs look good. I got the distinct impression I had wasted their precious time.

For Sifrey, and others like him, to give supermarket tabloids credit for generating a news story or for doing any valid reporting was unthinkable. But not long after the Palm Beach case, a supermarket tabloid broke another big story—Gennifer Flowers' explicit confession that she had sex with Bill Clinton. This time mainstream media didn't try to squirm away from the tabs. Instead, celebrity pundits explained why the tab stories were irrelevant and gave Clinton ample opportunity to deny the charges.

The real question today is not whether supermarket tabloids represent an influence on mainstream media, or even on politics at a gross level, but what sort of influence they have on the public mind.

If you include estimated "pass-along" reading rates, there are at least 50 million supermarket tabloid readers in America. Millions more absorb the headline messages while standing in line at the grocery store. The typical tabloid reader buys more than one tabloid at a time and reads no other newspaper, supplementing his or her views with television only.

Together, the six supermarket tabloids have a circulation of more than 10 million (compare this with 6.3 million of all Gannett papers combined). All six tabs concentrate editorial power into the hands of just two men: Mike Rosenbloom, owner of Globe Communications, and *National Enquirer* editor-in-chief Iain Calder, who carries out the will of American Media Inc. Globe Communications publishes the *Globe*, the *Sun* and the *National Examiner*. American Media, formerly Macfadden Holdings, publishes the *National Enquirer*, the *Star* and the *Weekly World News*.

To listen to the folks in the mainstream press and in the exalted halls of journalism schools one would think only numskulls read such rags. Except to ridicule tabloids, journalism schools don't even talk about them—they're so low on their scale. No classes are taught in tabloid writing or design. This billion-dollar publishing enterprise is dismissed and derided by illuminati who use "supermarket tabloid" as shorthand for anything frivolous, libelous, and dim-witted.

The function of journalism schools is not to teach reporting, and mainstream newspapers do not ferret out truth or even report "news." Establishment news outlets serve mostly to broadcast prevailing views of whomever is in charge and to make sure competing philosophies are dealt with quickly.

Educators are more in the business of churning out obedient citizens than in promoting the pursuit of knowledge. This is quite apparent in journalism schools, which churn out hordes of cookie sheet drones to man the memory holes at America's various propaganda enterprises. Budding students must be taught how to recognize authority and protect themselves against unapproved ideas. One of the best ways to neutralize an idea that challenges the status quo is to expose it to ridicule.

That tabloids are unbelievable is thought to be self-evident. So what do tabloids tell their readers? Tab stories often rely on such formulas as "miracle baby survives death plunge" or "the amazing garlic diet." Readers learn that a pitiful dog-baby was born in Romania, that vinegar can cure cancer, and that a lightning strike can transform a woman into a man.

Tabloids describe how foreigners in Muslim countries are routinely flogged and executed for trivial crimes. Tabloids denounce "druggies," who deserve life in prison, if not the death penalty, and expose homeless people as secret millionaires. Readers get helpful hints for how to silence nagging wives: Super-glue their mouths shut.

"MUST THIS GIRL DIE!?" screams a *Globe* headline, "while government money that could save her life is going to illegal aliens?" Just how the illegal aliens were depriving the girl of a liver transplant is never explained, but that doesn't matter. In the tabloid world, nonwhite foreigners are mocked and denigrated. The *Weekly World News* reports on 22 April 1997, "Kooky North Korean President Kim Jong II has his heart set on immigrating to the United States and marrying the girl of his dreams—tubby talk-show hostess Rosie O'Donnell!" The Japanese try to buy the Statue of Liberty and install it on Mount Fuji; African and South American tribesmen engage in painful religious rites; and third-world girls give birth at age six (when they're not being raised by wild animals).

The *Examiner* called Arabs "camel jockeys" in one of its pre-Gulf War headlines. The *Sun* ran photos of hanged Arabs, supposedly executed for drinking alcohol (even though the signs in Arabic around their necks accused them of spying—minor detail). The same issue ran a story about Chinese people with the headline "No Tickee, No Shirtee" written in chopstick-type strokes.

Tabloids serve the prevailing establishment view in ways network TV cannot. Only tabloids can get away with fabricating stories that deliberately slander evangelist preachers and Islam, or link various American "enemies" with Adolf Hitler and horrific plots to take over the world. During the Cold War—and even after the fall of the Berlin Wall—tabloids painted "Communists" as the most devious and ferocious of enemies. Eastern Bloc countries routinely served as the location for many fake stories about backward, lummox-like people who sold family members or otherwise defied civilization.

To produce such enticing articles week after week, tabloids need good people on staff. Talented, savvy people are in charge of the tabloids, and some have political connections. While a congressional aide in the 1960s, Phil Brennan secretly worked for Bill Buckley's *National Review*. Brennan originated that publication's famous "Cato" column of insider's info and speculations from the capital. Afterward, Brennan went to work for the *Enquirer* and later for the *National Examiner*, where he stamped a right-wing, Roman Catholic spin on his stories.

Still, tabloids are supposedly of no consequence to the establishment. *Newsweek* placed them at "the bottom of the media food chain." Tabloid editors do nothing to dispute those beliefs. Instead, they encourage outsiders to view them as inept liars who are constantly being sued. Whenever outsiders are permitted into tabloid offices, they seem to always fall for this snow job. Tabloid readers are exposed to an almost backward worldview that seems quaint, but is potentially dangerous. They rely on these publications as their main source of news and opinion, supplemented only by television. By studying the reading material of perhaps a quarter or more of the population, we can examine the American psyche and monitor the propaganda fed to it.

◆ ◆ ◆

1

The Tabloid Primordial Soup

Although the word *tabloid* refers only to a particular size of news-paper, in the 1950s and '60s it began to mean a sensationalistic newspaper full of sex, "gore" and bizarre tales of human behavior. As transmitters of gossip, tabloids are bound up with issues of social control. Tabloids are also about the fear of death and sex. They expose secrets and create or placate people's anxieties about the world around them. Information is power and to know something, especially to know something "forbidden," is to increase leverage over others.

In medieval towns and villages, the local priest held the most power because he knew more of the secret activities of the town's inhabitants than anyone else. In the confessional, he became privy to information that gave him an influence stronger than what he already wielded by having a say-so over a person's entry into heaven. In this way the church concentrated its power by reaching into even the smallest spheres of human activity. The pope had a fairly direct line to and from every part of his empire and could monitor political and social situations with a great degree of accuracy.

As always, gossip was disseminated by one or two people known to have good sources of information. Villagers were also fond of stories known as "fabliaux." Fabliaux entertained Europeans for hundreds of years before the invention of printing in that continent. Often sung in ballad form, such stories told of lives gone wrong, horrible accidents resulting in the loss of limbs, mistaken identities and, of course, sex and murder. Around the 15th century, when widespread use of printing came about in Europe, these ballads remained the basic form of the popular newspaper. As late as the 1870s in New York, printed ballads were on sale in city streets.

The supermarket tabloid can trace its roots to broadsides, which appeared in the early 17th century. These often appeared in ballad form on single printed sheets and covered such items as "The two Inseparable Brothers—or a true and strange description of a Gentleman (Italian by birth) about seventeene yeeres of age, who hath an imperfect (yet living) Brother, growing out of his side, having a head, two armes, and one leg, all perfectly to be seen."

A 1661 broadside tells the tragic tale of a man accidentally buried alive for three days. Other stories told of fires and plagues, mysterious happenings and strange births—like a pig born with a dolphin's face.

"A monstrous shape" or "a shapeless monster" theme appeared in print at the start of the 15th century, after being sung in villages for ages. The start of one reads, "A Description of a female creature borne in Holland, compleat in every part, save only a head like a swine, who have travailed into many parts, and is now to be scene in London. Shees loving, courteous, and effimenate, and here as yet could find a loving mate." The theme's not much different than that of a supermarket tab's tragic story of the "Crocodile Woman" who, despite her ugliness, is still a sweet soul desiring only of a loving husband.

Other proto-newspapers covered strictly business matters and confined their circulation to those who needed specific information. These missives descended in part from the ancient Roman letter-writing tradition that kept consuls around the world informed of the happenings in the Senate. These reports were expected to be sober and accurate accounts of truly important proceedings. One Roman consul at Cicilia, Turkey, complained of getting too much insignificant news—such as accounts of petty trials and gladiatorial contests. The letter writers continued to fill their missives with such "twiddle twaddle" anyway—knowing full well that their readers were dying to know.

During the Middle Ages and the Renaissance, Italian businessmen circulated handwritten newspapers to key subscribers in and out of Italy. Though handwritten, the newspapers still enjoyed a large circulation because of the bevy of scribes who cranked out copies.

By the early 17th century, when newspapers had spread to England, coffeehouses were the focal point of news dissemination. Both printed and handwritten newspapers, or newsbooks, told of ships' arrivals and cargo. Newsbooks also carried information we might consider outlandish today, but was of utmost importance to anyone involved in world commerce. Thus a 1576 report from France mentions "a monstrous and frightful serpent" found on the island of Cuba. Crucial news, indeed, for anyone involved in trade to the Caribbean.

Broadsheets describing "sensational" news enjoyed the largest circulation and have most influenced modern journalism. English broadsheets told not only of commercial "newes com from Italie," but also intriguing accounts such as "Tydings of a Huge and Ougly childe borne at Arnheim in Gelederland" and reports of talking ghosts, calves, pigeons and other animals. They published realistic accounts of murders, executions and other gruesome punishments doled out to transgressors. Child killers, cannibals, witches and stories of naked savages from the New World were staples as were details of their crimes and trials.

A MOST
Certain, Strange, and true Difcovery of a
VVITCH.
Being taken by fome of the Parliament Forces, as fhe was ftanding on a fmall planck board and fayling on it over the River of *Newbury*:

Together with the ftrange and true manner of her death, with the propheticall words and fpeeches fhe vfed at the fame time.

Printed by John Hammond, 1643.

Over time, broadsheets became standardized and gave rise to the first newspaper publishers. One of the first regularly published broadsheets was called the *Newgate Calendar*, published in London by Jemmy Catnach's Seven Dials Press. Catnach branched his publishing empire out to Liverpool, Manchester, Hull, Sheffield, Durham, and a slew of other provincial towns.

Catnach's successful broadsheet formula focused on accounts from London's Newgate Prison. The inexpensive handbills gave readers titillating accounts of condemned prisoners' last words, their tearful or defiant confessions, and their horrible end. The method of execution often depended on the whim of the executioner or was based on the gravity of a person's crime. People could be burned at the stake or be forced to hold bags of gunpowder under their arms or between their legs. These bags would burst into searing flame, prolonging the agony of the condemned instead of speeding his death. Woodcuts depicting such deaths (or more interestingly, the flogging of a group of naked nuns in Russia!) often accompanied such accounts.

Catnach found that while gossip was steadily and eagerly consumed by his readers, nothing claimed their attention as well as a good disaster. "Fires are our best friends next to murders," he said, "if they're *good* fires. . . . There's no great chance of any more great buildings being burned; worse luck. People don't care much about private fires. A man in the street don't heed so much who's burnt to death in the next [house]. . . .

"The fire at Ben Caunt's, where the poor children was burnt to hashes, was the best of the private house fires that I've worked, I think. I made four shillings on it, one day. He was the champion once, and away at a fight at the time, and it was a shocking thing so people bought." As today, a tragedy befalling a celebrity is far more popular than one striking even one's next-door neighbor.

The oral storytelling tradition of modifying stock tales continued into the age of the printing press. Like today's tabloids, broadsheet publishers were not above inventing a little news on a slow day. Known as "cocks" or "catchpennies," the fake stories reveal what captured people's attention in the 16th century. Many stories were recycled continually with only a few changes added to make them "new."

Catnach and other publishers could have been shut down by the authorities at any time. Books and other printed material were strictly controlled. Anything printed was presumed to be illegal unless a specific license was granted by the Crown or another suitable authority. Whatever appeared in these publications needed at least tacit approval of the establishment.

None of these papers ever challenged the authority of the king, or if they did, they were soon stopped and their presses seized. The rulers kept a close watch over those whose voices could shape public opinion.

Not only the reading material of the past, but also its politics have remained essentially the same through the centuries. When asked what might have happened had his tabloids opposed the Gulf War, Phil Bunton, editorial director of Globe Communications, said, "We would have lost money hand over fist." He may very well be right. Opposing the government has never been a good way to get rich.

Bringing News to the Street

The market for newspapers had to be broadened to include people literate enough to read one but, for whatever reason, were not viewed as potential readers. In the late 1800s Horace Day pioneered the "penny press." Day took his daily paper, the *New York Sun,* and sold it for a penny to people who had been ignored by "respectable" newspapers. In England, a prohibitive stamp tax on all newspapers had driven their price beyond what a regular worker could afford. In America, the absence of such a tax allowed the general public to peruse the paper's engaging accounts of crimes and women gone bad.

Day borrowed the newsboy tradition from the English press and used it to promote his paper in the States. Until the early 1830s, American papers were sold by subscription only. By hiring newsboys to hawk the paper at street corners, Day made the paper that much more accessible.

It was into this tumultuous world of newsboys calling out the most sensationalistic headlines the editors could dream up that Bernarr Macfadden stepped. The first tabloid-sized paper appeared in the early 1920s, and in 1924 Macfadden's *New York Evening Graphic* became one of the first to exploit the advantages of this format. The tabloid focused on printing images and required less reading time or ability from its readers. If a picture paints a thousand words, readers could gobble down far more news in just a glance than anyone reading the text-dense *New York Times.* (The word *tabloid* comes from the same root as *tablet* and means "easy to swallow.") Tabloid-sized papers were much easier to handle than the sail-like broadsheets, meant to be read in a quiet home.

Macfadden's success came from mixing the popular first-person "confessional" magazines with the exciting news of the day. He told his editors, "Don't stick with the bare skeleton of facts." He also invented the "composograph"—altered photos. News constituted anything that could grab and hold readers' attentions long enough to get them to buy the paper. Like today's supermarket tabs, these papers had to sell themselves every issue. Failure to deliver on the promise of titillating "news" could mean the permanent loss of a reader. In these papers we find the genesis of the modern headline and see its importance in all newspapers to the present.

In America, some of the greatest names in the holy art of journalism got their start by continuing the tradition of the sensationalistic broadside. In the late 1800s, William Randolph Hearst established a huge, influential publishing empire whose papers specialized in inflammatory text geared toward mass appeal. It's well-known that the power of the press belongs to whomever owns it. Hearst's famous quote, "You give me the pictures, gentlemen, and I'll give you a war," proved true.

Hearst didn't really need pictures to start a war. All he had to do was engineer the explosions aboard the *USS Maine* harbored in Spanish-controlled Cuba to help bring about the Spanish-American War in 1898. The bogus attack was just the excuse needed by the United States to attack and occupy Spanish colonies throughout the world. To shore up public opinion that a war was needed, Hearst's papers laid on the propaganda, even to the point of using the forbidden word *murder* in a headline.

"Yellow journalism" has come to mean the biased, jingoistic promotion of war and other American interests and the deliberately distorted but eye-catching stories about crime and vice. The standard-bearers of yellow journalism, Alfred Pulitzer's *New York World* and Hearst's *New York Journal*, competed fiercely. Some of their greatest battles took place during the Spanish-American War, when both papers would sometimes give up the entire front page to inflammatory headlines. Both papers ran fake stories illustrated by stock photos. Neither paper was averse to sensationalizing even the most pedestrian of stories to sell their papers more quickly.

True Confessions

The closest relatives of the supermarket tabloid are the scandal and "confession" magazines and tabloids, which showed up in the '30s and hit their stride from the '50s to the early '70s. The end of World War II created a different market for pulp publishers. Not only had soldiers developed a taste for pin-up girls and sex stories, but their war experiences had hardened them to what we now refer to as gore. In addition, blacks and women had gained a chunk of autonomy as a result of the war economy and were recognized as a lucrative market of their own.

As Alan Betrock points out in his seminal work *Unseen Culture: The Roots of Cult,* the wartime paper restrictions helped increase the popularity of this new literature. Publishers had to use lower quality paper and issue their publications in smaller sizes. The restrictions on paper were not fully lifted until 1950. Once that had happened, a flood of cheap paper hit the market and thousands of new publications sprang up.

Many of these publications never intended to get past the first issue. Known as "one-shots," they cashed in on the celebrity of a certain star, exploited a certain fad, or exposed a particular "crime wave." It was all titillation. Opium rings and "white slave" markets were forever being dredged up. Tales of violence, crime and women in jeopardy became so commonplace the sight of a terrified female—bound and gagged on the cover—became cliché. Like the medieval fabliaux, these stories appealed to basic fears, including society's fear of women. Just as common as the tied-up damsel in distress was the crazy-eyed murderess about to plunge an ice pick into some hapless man's heart.

In 1952 the magazine *Confidential* became such a sudden success that it changed the face of the genre. *Confidential's* inventor and publisher was Robert Harrison, who had already put out a number of "girlie" titles, including *Eyeful, Whisper* and *Titter.* His formula focused on celebrities, mercilessly rummaging through their closets. The publication also contained stories that accented ordinary fears of ordinary people, such as unemployment, "Will a Robot Take Your Job?" and race-mixing, "What Makes Eartha Kitt a White Man's Darling?"

Race was always a heavy issue in these publications, as it is today. At the same time *Confidential* and its competitors created their markets, magazines geared toward blacks sprang up. With names like *Copper* and *Sepia*, their formulas duplicated their white counterparts, except they stressed race a bit more and a bit more forcefully: "Ava Gardner—Dark Men in Her Bed Chamber."

Harrison's *Confidential* owed a lot of its success to the sheer ruthlessness with which its reporters gathered facts. It was the first magazine to employ long-range lenses, hidden microphones and tape recorders, and even strong-arm techniques to squeeze information from reluctant sources. Harrison popularized the use of outlandishly doctored photos and creative cutting and pasting of existing photos to create photo collages that further damned their targets.

Such a magazine could not piss off so many rich people without paying a price. By 1958, Harrison was forced to abandon *Confidential* under the weight of the many lawsuits filed by celebrities whose lives had been opened up in the pages of the magazine. *Confidential* lurched on under other publishers and with different editorial slants until the early 1970s, although it was never the same.

Throughout the '60s pulp magazines stratified into clear categories, some specializing in romance, others in detective stories or true crime. Some brought the public lurid stories of all-night Hollywood orgies, dope slaves and hints of homosexuality. Anxiety about gender, as always, was a proven seller, and these mags had their share of "I Am Changing into a Man" stories. Although the photographs and outright sex pornography were tame by today's standards, it is hard to say the same for their topics.

While today it may be de rigueur for a magazine to show a woman's nipples or to graphically describe any and all sexual acts, it would be hard to match the older magazines for their implied hedonism and fetishism. Headlines promised stories of "My Secret Shame" or "Cuba's Legalized Filth." Others hinted at rapes resulting in either marriage or suicide. Nazi women, too, made their debut here, with leather-strapped women either hanging by manacles and chains or brandishing a curling whip before red walls draped with huge swastikas. And what are we to make of a story called "Repented Lover," accompanied by a photograph of a woman thrusting her cleavage before the camera's lens? The reader's mind is left to contemplate the unsaid and unspeakable.

During this era Generoso Pope launched the *National Enquirer* (originally the *New York Enquirer*). His tabloid newspaper blended exploitation, grotesque photo-reporting and gossipy advice columns. Purchased in 1952 as an unloved stepchild in the Hearst newspaper empire, the *Enquirer* had a circulation of just 75,000, which languished at that figure for the next eight years. In 1960, Pope changed the name of his paper to *National Enquirer* and set the standard and tone for all other supermarket tabloids.

Mainstream vs. Tab Content

The history of news publishing takes us from an oral tradition to such modern publications as the *National Enquirer* and the *U.S. News and World Report*. Both the *National Enquirer* and the *U.S. News and World Report* contain essentially the same things: stories that interpret the world around us. Gee whiz. Supermarket tabs are anything but maverick. At most they provide a false sense of "extreme" by which we may pretend to judge other forms of newscasting. But the measure is an illusion. Although it is common to present the tabs as using unacceptable means to gather and report news, they have done nothing of the sort. Even in the last few decades, when pulp and tabloid journalism have been relegated to a ghetto, similarities with the mainstream press are far more striking than their differences.

For all its pretensions, the establishment press is dependent on the same tools for investigating, writing and marketing its product. In 1972 the *New York Times* devoted editorial space to decry the *National Enquirer's* digging through Henry Kissinger's trash to find clues as to what the powerful "statesman" was up to. This opinion was printed just one year after the *Times* had printed the now-famous Pentagon Papers, documents admittedly stolen from the State Department.

Nevertheless, tabloids are regarded by many as unbelievable compared to the mainstream media. There is little evidence to support this.

Leafing through any tabloid, a reader would find the same phrases used by the *New York Times* to buttress its opinions: "government sources say," "sources close to the President revealed," or the ever-popular "in documents obtained by." If "inside sources" are regarded as credible in the *Washington Post*, why not in the *Weekly World News*? And so what if the source is faked? The blurring between fact and fiction is essential in both mainstream and tabloid press. The only difference is the tabloids don't claim to be the Final Truth on anything.

After all, it was the *New York Times* and not the *National Enquirer* that reported the Tawana Brawley case as gospel. It was the *Washington Post*, not the *Sun*, that gave us the Pulitzer-Prize-winning "Jimmy's World" by Janet Cooke. Bob Woodward, Cooke's editor and originator of Deep Throat, that most famous anonymous source, didn't bother to see if there was a real 8-year-old junkie to match the boy in the story, so why should we?

Yet supermarket tabloids may be the last form of real reporting and real journalism left. These days the mainstream press meekly accepts— even endorses—"pool reporting" with Pentagon censors and relies so heavily on press releases and other manufactured news they can be hoaxed almost at will. Journalism schools have begun to proliferate, ensuring a guild-like adherence to the prevailing party line. Those reporters who stray from approved subjects, express controversial opinions or otherwise question their betters are quickly weeded out. Mainstream newspapers now rely on these journalism programs to send them acceptable drones who will not act up or otherwise cause problems for the paper.

Thus, a reporter for the *Chicago Tribune* who dutifully repeats whatever a policeman tells him or who rewords a press release dropped onto his desk has become the norm. A tabloid reporter who stakes out a scene or who poses as a window cleaner to get a look inside someone's office is considered somehow sleazy.

In the 1980s and '90s the so-called "mainstream press" has fallen even more in line with the supermarket tabloids as they elbowed their way into the checkout lines, changing their cover formats to compete.

Time and *Newsweek* are sold next to the *Weekly World News* and their covers are at times indistinguishable. Prozac, O.J. Simpson, suicide cult Heaven's Gate and liquid diets have all adorned the covers of these respectable magazines. Even the staid *Reader's Digest* has taken to printing tear-off covers with the words *SEX* or *DIET* in 48-point type.

If there were ever any doubt about the blurring between mainstream and "trash" journalism, it was dispelled when Time Inc. joined the fray to buy the *National Enquirer* when it came up for sale in 1988.

Nine years later, *Time* chose Steve Coz, editor of the *National Enquirer*, as one of the 25 most influential people of the year. The magazine praises the tabloids' dedicated coverage of national scandals: "In stories ranging from the Dick Morris scandal to the JonBenet Ramsey murder case, the *Enquirer* and its fellow tabloids have been out front, while much of the mainstream media follow." *Time* can't get away without an insult, though, adding a fallacious bit that the *Enquirer's* publishes stories about UFOs and ghosts.

♦ ♦ ♦

2

Shocking! Incredible! Secrets of Tabloids Revealed

Anyone looking for a tabloid exposé is bound to be disappointed because there is really nothing to expose about the tabloids. Every news organization or reporter who has tried to do it has failed.

Do tabloids make up stories? Sure they do. That's not a secret anymore than it's a secret that *NBC News* faked an exploding pickup truck. Do they pay money? Yep. And so do other papers—just not as much (the *NYT* paid a janitor $200 for a file on Jeffrey Dahmer for instance, or so says the janitor, so denies the *New York Times*).

Are tabloids ruthless with each other, even within their own organizations? You bet your boots they are. Ask Stuart Goldman, an experienced investigative reporter who set out to infiltrate then expose the lurid and seamy world of tabloid journalism. In the end he found himself living in a web of lies more grotesque than anything he had imagined he would find. He was a quadruple—maybe a quintuple—agent making a spiffy living by "spying" on tabloids and tabloid TV shows. To do this he had to become one of them and then, in his own words, something worse: a snitch.

And as snitches have long been treated, he was hunted down and damn near ruined by those he betrayed. After a year or two selling out his various employers, he found himself facing felony charges for illegally accessing computers for the purpose of stealing stories to sell to competitors. He'd been set up, took the bait and his primary foes, found at Fox Broadcasting, meant to make an example out of him.

They did. After more than a year of prosecution, the disintegration of his marriage and the near-loss of his sanity, he pleaded guilty to three of the counts and got probation, restitution and community service. He felt very lucky not to have gone to jail. He fought the sentence for more than three years before he was able to have it dismissed. A hollow victory if there ever was one. But a good object lesson in tabloid journalism.

These people are not kidding around. Tabloid journalism is tough and it is cut-throat. They may be having fun at it, but they take it very seriously. Anyone interested in truly studying journalism should too.

The Big Six

To deconstruct tabloids and their sociopolitical meaning, we first have to define the terms of study. This book focuses on *supermarket* tabloids, and not just any tabloid-sized newspaper, which could be the *Christian Science Monitor* as well as the *Weekly World News*. Supermarket tabs are published weekly and are printed mostly in color. Unlike big-city tabloids like the *New York Post*, they don't try to cover local breaking news. But they do share a penchant for sensational news stories, played up with huge, blunt headlines, such as the *Post*'s "KITTY DUKAKIS DRANK RUBBING ALCOHOL." Supermarket tabloids can be very good sources of news in the truest sense of the word—information you haven't heard before.

The six major tabs often get lumped together in the public mind, which makes them that much harder to study. The *National Enquirer* has become to tabloids what Kleenex is to facial tissue. However, there are striking differences between the tabs, and each has a peculiar history.

Generoso Pope bought the *National Enquirer* in 1952. For the first decade or so, gore took center stage. Big headlines blared, "Passion Pills Fan Rape Wave" and "Madman Cut Up His Date and Put Her Body in His Freezer." Looking back at the early days, Pope said, "We ran a lot of gore purely because I noticed that people used to congregate around accident scenes. That's not something we're proud of." In 1968 Pope decided to break into the checkout stands, and the magazine became more wholesome.

The *Weekly World News* was created in 1980 after the *Enquirer* went color and publisher Generoso Pope didn't want to sell his black-and-white press facility in Pompano Beach, Florida. The *WWN* took stories that didn't fit in the *Enquirer*, plus the weird foreign stories and those that must be pure fiction (from 15 April 1977, "Hell Found on Asteroid—And It's Headed Toward Us!"). Rafe Klinger, formerly of the *WWN*, stated, "The key to understanding tabloids is irreverence. Nobody is too sacred or too important to go after."

Today the tab is a cult organ for college students, with a circulation of about 1 million. The *Weekly World News* enthralls readers with nagging evidence of a World War II bomber found on the moon and wows them with an amazing marshmallow diet. The paper was edited for eight years by Joe West before he was suddenly fired. Now it is edited by Eddie Clontz, a former editor at the *St. Petersburg Times*.

To compete with the *WWN*, Globe Communications launched the *Sun*, which is color and contains a good measure of "wacky" stories (from 15 April 1997, "Sex-Change Woman Makes Self Pregnant" and "Ghost Throws Girls Across Room"). Since 1983 the *Sun* has built a circulation of between a half and three quarters of a million. Like the *WWN*, it's most popular among college students and bona fide insane people.

The *WWN* and the *Sun* are the tabloids most often cited whenever someone in the mainstream seeks to denigrate them. When Bill

Clinton was caught by the *Star* in his 12-year affair with Gennifer Flowers, he tried to get out of it by reminding us that the *Star* also ran stories of Martians and the "cow-faced boy." He was completely wrong.

The *Star* has never run such stories. Its contents are almost indistinguishable from that of *People* or many parts of *Time*. The *Star* employs crack attorneys and reporters to ensure its allegations are true. Confining itself largely to the celebrity beat, the *Star* has to make sure its facts are correct and will hold up under close scrutiny. Hollywood celebrities and state governors have a great deal of legal weapons at their disposal, and to libel just one of them could put a tab out of business for good (as has happened to more than one tabloid).

Rupert Murdoch began the *Star* in 1974, no doubt inspired by the success of the *Enquirer*. By 1990, when the *Star* was sold to the *Enquirer*'s owners for $400 million, the tab had a weekly readership of around 3.6 million. The *Star* has always claimed it is not a supermarket tabloid like the *Enquirer*. It has sought to distance itself from the image, preferring to be grouped with more upstanding publications like *People*. The difference has always been academic to begin with, since all these publications are sold in supermarket checkout lines and often have identical cover stories.

The *Globe* is often placed third behind the celebrity-oriented *Enquirer* and *Star*, although it's the flagship of Globe Communications. To differentiate itself, the *Globe* tries to be more daring and more willing to go with a story before it's absolutely buttoned down. When editor Wendy Henry ran the picture and name of the alleged rape victim at the Kennedy compound in Palm Beach, the rest of the media went into a tizzy. The publication landed in a Florida court for violating a 1911 state law prohibiting the publication of rape victims' names. The case was eventually thrown out, but not after substantial cost and headache to the owners of the paper. This victory for the free press went unheralded by the rest of the media.

But it sold papers.

The *Globe* has covered numerous salacious stories that other tabs ignored, including allegations that Bill Clinton fathered a child of a black prostitute and that former California Governor Jerry Brown held satanic orgies upstairs during fund-raisers for his presidential campaign. Although the *Enquirer* broke the news that Rock Hudson had AIDS, the *Globe* countered with sleazy tales recounting the movie star's habit of picking up young guys for wild one-night stands.

The *National Examiner*, which has a circulation that fluctuates between 800,000 and 1.5 million, is the odd man out. It seems to be a running experiment for Globe Communications. Its budget is relatively low, so it cannot afford to buy the gossip that is the stock and trade of the celebrity tabs. It has enough backing, though, to cover certain events and to pay stringers to phone in information.

The *Examiner* is a supermarket tab in the old style of the '60s. Not often relying on celebrity stories or far-fetched drama, the *Examiner* is a traditional mix of heart-warming true adventures and pro-wrestling news. However, the *Examiner*, like all the tabs, is always changing. At times, various editors of the *Examiner* have forbidden fabricated stories known as "top-of-the-heads" or "wing-its," which are the bread and butter of the *Weekly World News* and the *Sun*. But the temptation to buff up a good story idea is too great to make a "TOH" ban stick for long at the *Examiner*.

The *Globe* is not above plundering the *Examiner* for juicy stories. The *Examiner* once sent reporter Bob Boyd to Washington, D.C., to comb through the FBI files of famous people. He developed an interesting series of articles—among them tidbits about Marilyn Monroe's political dalliances and John Wayne's role as an FBI informant. *Examiner* editor Billy Burt carelessly left some of the materials on his desk while he was out of the office, and *Globe* editor Paul Levy began rifling through it. He insisted that such good stuff belonged in the *Globe* and pitched a bitch. The *Examiner* was forced to give up some of the best stories to appease Levy.

Periodically, great firing purges clear out entire newsrooms. The mass exoduses help shape the direction a tabloid takes. After each coup, editors assert their power by adding, changing or killing stories just to show they can—much as Levy did by taking the *Examiner*'s FBI stories. Levy, who had been canned from his $180,000 job at the *Enquirer* as soon as Generoso Pope died, had to "prove" himself worthy all over again at the *Globe*.

The Cover

Supermarket tabloids suffer the "Scheherazade Syndrome," based on the dilemma of the princess in the *Thousand and One Nights*. Each night she has to deliver such a compelling story that she will avoid execution the next morning, so she may continue the drama the next evening. Like the princess, tabloid editors face enormous pressure each time they tell their stories. Even a single low-selling issue is a blot on an editor's history and not easily erased.

Daily newspapers make the majority of their money from advertisers and can depend on a substantial number of sales to subscribers. Unlike daily newspapers, supermarket tabloids rely on the cover price for at least 80% of their profits. Ad revenues for supermarket tabs are low, ranging from around 16% to 20%. Tabs are far more dependent on selling each issue each time to each person.

Every week, tabloid editors are forced to gamble their careers. With that constant pressure, editors use the cover as their most powerful tool. "It may look like garbage but that's the way we want it to look," said Cliff Linedecker, former assistant editor at the *National Examiner*. "We always tried to make the cover look like a circus poster."

Although tabloids have commissioned marketing surveys and focus groups, tabloid editors like to rely on their guts to tell them what works and what doesn't. They break a buyer's habits into tiny pieces, looking for any opportunity to snare a sale. There is always a difference between the tabs—even differences within the same title from issue to issue—as each tabloid strives to catch the eye of the reader.

Typical Tabloid Cover

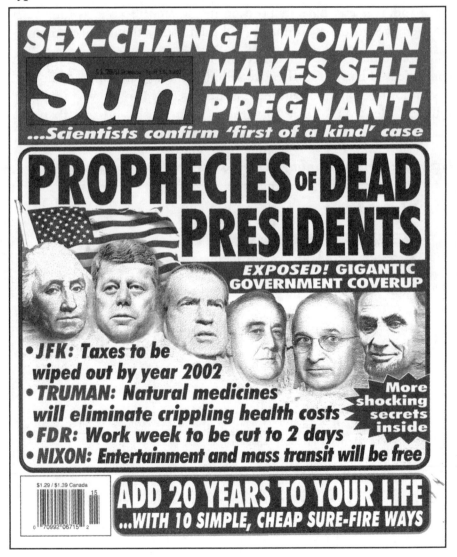

Bob Smith, former editor of the *Star* and the *Enquirer*, said, "I've read all these marketing surveys, and they always talk about the key thing that sells a tabloid is the impulse buy. But I find that's ranked number three. The first thing is availability—is it in the supermarket in the first place and, if it is, what's its position in the rack? Second is impact. If it's there, it's gotta have impact. And then comes the impulse to buy.

"Impulse buys make up something like 30% of all the buys," Smith continued. "That's a lot. If you're selling 4 million and 30% is impulse, if you don't get any impulse buying that week you're down to 2.7, 2.8 million. Then you'll fill it up with an Elvis Presley picture, then you find they're buying—and there's an impulse buy increase of 100%!"

Interoffice Memo Regarding Tabloid Sales and Rack Positioning

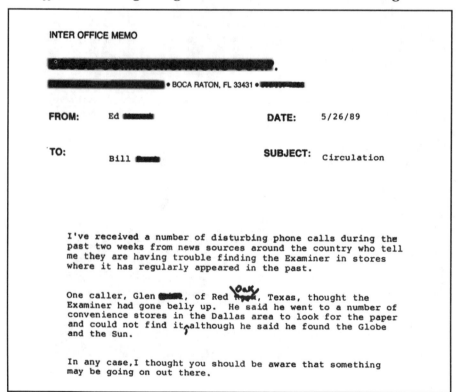

INTER OFFICE MEMO

▮▮▮▮▮▮▮▮▮▮▮▮▮▮▮▮▮▮▮▮▮▮▮▮▮.

▮▮▮▮▮▮▮▮▮▮▮ • BOCA RATON, FL 33431 • ▮▮▮▮▮▮▮

FROM: Ed ▮▮▮▮▮   DATE: 5/26/89

TO: Bill ▮▮▮▮   SUBJECT: Circulation

I've received a number of disturbing phone calls during the past two weeks from news sources around the country who tell me they are having trouble finding the Examiner in stores where it has regularly appeared in the past.

One caller, Glen ▮▮▮▮, of Red Oak, Texas, thought the Examiner had gone belly up. He said he went to a number of convenience stores in the Dallas area to look for the paper and could not find it, although he said he found the Globe and the Sun.

In any case, I thought you should be aware that something may be going on out there.

Eye level is the optimum rack position, and tabloids pay a premium to occupy this space. Tabloids employ people to spot-check supermarkets around the country to make sure the tabs are getting what they pay for, and to make sure the competition hasn't usurped a certain position. These same guys aren't above repositioning a few stacks of tabs themselves.

Former *National Examiner* editor Billy Burt started as a ruthless Fleet Street reporter, skillfully lifting family pictures during interviews at the homes of people struck by tragedy. He was fired during a 1990 coup but came back to power as a "super consultant" for the *Enquirer*, developing new publications and writing quickie books on celebrities. Burt is famous for his insights into the cover. While at the *Examiner*, the walls of his office were thick with stapled covers of every past issue in chronological order. He flipped through them constantly, developing a feel for what worked and what didn't.

Despite his efforts, he admitted it's hopeless to predict the success of an issue by the cover. He couldn't explain why a Liz Taylor story may sell very well one week, then not work at all two weeks later. "You just sit back, put your feet up and watch the covers," Burt said. "You're never gonna latch onto a trend, but at least you're gonna learn what not to do again."

As Burt explained, such devotion to the cover is necessary because "it's the only selling point you have. It's your only promotion billboard; it's your only selling point, unless you're gonna spend millions on television advertising or send out a PR team to promote your story, but tabloids don't have that."

The *National Examiner*, with its million-plus circulation, has never had more than 23,000 people subscribing—despite the substantial discount for doing so. It's that way at all the tabloids. Marketing studies show that most tabloid buyers do not intend to purchase one before arriving in the checkout line and spend fewer than four seconds looking at a cover before deciding to buy. A cover can be rejected in a second. Studies in which lasers were aimed at customer's eyes reveal that a person's gaze does not often drop below the top half of the page. Sometimes it goes no further than the title.

Tabloid covers no longer contain page numbers next to the stories. If a potential buyer picks up a tab because of an intriguing headline, the editors don't want that person to flip to the correct page, quickly read the story and put it back. Tabloid stories are not known for their length and rely heavily on pictures. It's not like the *Wall Street Journal*, where a readers must devote a significant amount of time to a story if they mean to read it.

Page numbers would also break up the flow of the paper's look. "Tabs don't put page numbers on the covers because it slows it down and spoils the totality of the thing," Burt commented. "The front page is the whole you're interested in. It's all very well and good having a 'must-buy' headline, but you want the whole thing to gel. There's probably gonna be four stories on that page and maybe three pictures. There's gonna be a logo and you want the whole thing to harmonize."

Exhaustive examinations of cover stories have yielded very little concrete data. In the end it is the editor's instincts that must come up with the answer.

Headlines

The paper might look haphazard, but the formula is exacting. A "gee-whiz" is the banner headline at the top that announces a 7-year-old girl had a baby on a rollercoaster. "Hey, Marthas" are stories that combine impact with the ability to hold a reader's interest. In tabloid circles these win as much praise as Pulitzer-winning articles in the mainstream press. The classic "Hey, Martha!" story is "Headless Body Found in Topless Bar."

Also crucial to a good cover is a "must-buy" headline. "People see a headline like 'Marilyn Monroe Was a Dyke!' and say, 'Aw, Christ, I gotta buy that one,'" *Examiner*'s Billy Burt said. "Every editor every week sits down and tries to come up with a 'must-buy' headline that'll catch people's attention."

The "must-buy" is not always obvious, and tabloid editors sometimes have to make tough editorial calls that can mean the gain or loss of

---

"Gee-Whiz" Headlines

Star, 22 April 1997

Sun, 15 April 1997

"Hey, Martha!" Headlines

Weekly World News, 15 April 1997

Sun, 8 April 1997

"Must-Buy" Headlines

National Examiner, 15 April 1997

Sun, 19 March 1991

hundreds of thousands of sales, not to mention their jobs. They don't waste time philosophizing on whether or not their journalistic "ethics" are offended.

"Can you imagine sitting at an editorial conference and you got the 'Monkey Business' picture, with Donna Rice sittin' on Gary Hart's knee?" asked tabloid editor Bob Smith. "I wasn't involved in that one, but can you imagine sitting at that conference saying, 'Will we use that picture big on page one, or will we crop it to postage stamp size and put a teaser—'Shocking Exclusive Picture Inside'?' Now will that sell more, or will they buy it because it's on the cover? That's a typical 'must-buy' situation, but it's also a pretty hard judgment call."

It's worth taking a closer look at how headlines are perceived by readers, especially since headlines are even more important to tabloids than to mainstream newspapers. Many newspaper readers go no further than reading the headline. Moreover, the headline seems to influence readers' thinking even if the article's text does not support it, and even if it *contradicts* it.

"People have a tendency to interpret what they hear in ways that are bigger than what the statement itself conveys," explained Deborah Gruenfeld of the University of Illinois. Gruenfeld found that the content—whether it supported the headline or contradicted it—had the same effect in either diminishing or increasing a preformed belief in the headline.

In Gruenfeld's 1990 study, participants read the seemingly neutral headline "Black Democrats Supported Jesse Jackson for President in 1988," then rated the statement as true or untrue on a scale of 1 to 10, with 10 being absolute truth. Astonishingly, participants who read statements that supported the headline and participants who read statements that contradicted it both dropped to almost the same level of disbelief. The troubling conclusion is that headline readers tend to believe a headline, and that any further information merely erodes their belief.

University of Virginia researcher Daniel Wegner phrased headlines in the form of denials, questions and accusations to see what effect each variation might have on the reader. Wegner found that people who read the accusatory headline "Smith Took Bribes" were less likely to believe it than those who got the information as "Did Smith Take Bribes?" Phrasing the headline as a denial, "Smith Did Not Take Bribes," was most likely to be perceived as true, but not to any great degree. The numbers suggest that to deny something is only marginally less damaging than to admit it. And headlines tend to be believed in the first place.

Wegner compared reactions to fake headlines allegedly taken from the *Midnight Globe* and the *National Enquirer* and compared them to identical headlines he claimed were from the *New York Times* and the *Washington Post*. He found subjects more likely to believe the *Post* and the *Times* (4.65 on a scale of 1 to 7, where 7 is most believable) than the tabs (4.12). When headlines were phrased as questions, the believability quotient narrowed to 4.28 for the "respectable" papers and 3.97 for the supermarket tabs. When the headlines were phrased as denials, the results were identical.

These studies imply that people tend to believe what they read in a headline wherever and however they see it, even if the source is supposedly "disreputable" and even if the accompanying story refutes the headline. Mentioning two disparate items in a headline will link them in a reader's mind, where they are likely to stick. Those who don't bother to read the story retain the idea the most. And even those who read the story are not likely to be influenced by its facts.

These studies suggest that if people read tab headlines at all, which is almost impossible to avoid, that *not* reading the rest of the story makes the headlines more believable. The implications of spreading mass subliminal messages become enormous when tabloids are considered for their propaganda value.

The Guts

Filling the pages of a supermarket tabloid is a formulaic process and can be handled with an almost assembly-line approach. Staff writers typically crank out far more stories per week than appear in the paper to create a healthy backlog. Noncelebrity stories have lead times of at least three weeks. Even the most trivial of stories may go through a half-dozen rewrites before the editors are satisfied. *Nothing* appears in a tabloid story by accident.

Tabs' budgets may call for a certain percentage of Bigfoot stories, or a certain number and type of diet articles. Whenever a need arises, editors simply reach into a large file cabinet known as the bin and retrieve whatever story fits the hole they have to fill. If it's a 6-inch UFO story, it's there. If they need a 12-incher on a miracle cure at Lourdes, no problem.

As tab editor Burt suggested, there is no exact science to what goes into a tabloid, yet correct timing seems to play a role. Thus, vinegar and mayo diets might appear only twice a year. Even though Elvis is a proven seller, he cannot be reincarnated at will. The time must be ripe. It is only by measuring covers against each other that editors have found any way to anticipate their audience's interests—an audience made up of nonsubscribers acting on impulse.

Celebrity photos are guaranteed to appear in the same places in a tabloid, and the "mix" of stories is almost like a recipe, with certain genres appearing in certain places in the book. "Everybody keeps experimenting with the mix," Burt said, "but there are some things you know are good sellers, like diet stories, or a good medical story that affects everybody. That people can relate to. People are interested in that. And Bible stories are also a staple.

"The most popular tabloids—the *Star* and the *Enquirer*—they've gone beyond the mix. What better mix can you get than Michael Landon with cancer? Merv Griffin being gay? Kitty Kelly's book on Nancy Reagan? And the *Enquirer* adds a bonus about the Kennedy rape scandal on the cover! That's a mix of all that's good in celebrity tabloid journalism.

"Back in the 1970s there was the traditional tabloid mix of health, love, money, celebrity, plus the psychic bit. But it's changed. It's only since the tabloids started getting really good color that they really promoted the main picture, and now that's always a celebrity."

Burt recalled earlier days of tabloids when part of the mix was to feed off popular television shows. He felt it was one of the key components that made the *Enquirer* and others so successful. "That was when television was at its peak and you had the celebrities. You had *Charlie's Angels* and every week you could rotate Farrah Fawcett, Jaclyn Smith, Cheryl Ladd, Kate Jackson. Look at Joan Collins. *Dynasty* and all these major soaps had millions of people watch every week, and they really wanna know what's going on in the stars' lives. Do they fuck around like they do on the show?"

The arrival of cable TV has so diluted this once lucrative pool of recognizable celebrities that tabloids have had to work hard to find stars to take their places. But the pickings are slim. In the '80s and '90s "tabloid TV" began to reverse the trend and feed off the supermarket tabloids. Almost every day tabs are called up by producers of shows like *Hard Copy, Inside Edition* and *A Current Affair*. Ironically, calls come in just as often from the network news shows.

"The tabs used to feed off television. Now television's feeding off the tabloids. *Nightline*—Ted Koppel gets his best ratings, *20/20* gets their best ratings, when they do tabloid stories. Of course the greatest thing is to hold [the tabloid] up and say, 'Look at this piece of shit. We would never do a story like this.' And then they repeat the story!" Burt said.

"The *Examiner* once ran a story about Randy Travis possibly being gay. He was on *Entertainment Tonight* with Mary Hart, saying, 'I'm not gay,' but he gives them a full fuckin' interview. They show the cover of the paper and that says he *is* gay. They ask him if he is gay and he says he's *not* gay. But they perpetuate the whole bloody thing. If it's libel then what are they doing going around repeating the libel?!"

Because of the dearth of sure-selling TV characters, tabloids have had to search for their stories where they've always been—whatever interests the reader. Inevitably, readers turn to tabloids for comfort and titillation. They go there to be assured the world outside is worse than they can imagine and that, in the end, a humdrum life doesn't mean they're a failure. Consensus reality is really reality, after all.

3

Deconstruction of Tabloid Themes

Strictly defined morals are laid on thick in the tabs, where two-dimensional figures of good or evil are clearly delineated. Stories have obvious heroes and villains. Such stories serve to reassure the reader that "traditional values" still hold true and will win out in the end. Same goes for the Protestant "work ethic." Tabloids unfailingly trumpet the value of unstinting loyalty to employer and spouse. And the promised reward never fails to appear.

Even after grudgingly tipping their hats to the tabs for O.J. trial news, journalism school professors and their graduates insist the tabs exert no influence over mainstream media. Editors and publishers of newspapers all over America espouse the same opinion, even as they slavishly copy tabloid marketing techniques and layout designs and play catch-up to the latest stories. At most they concede the influence of *USA Today*, moaning about being forced to lower their standards to compete with the horrid "McNewspaper." In fact, *USA Today* has more in common with the *National Enquirer* than with the *Philadelphia Inquirer*. The tabs pioneered many popular features in *USA Today*, such as splashy color photos, snappy articles and ridiculous snippets of trivia cast as essential facts.

Flipping through mainstream newspapers, we see more than a little fluff: the horoscope, celebrity news, local gossip columns and cartoon pages. Dissecting a daily "newspaper" reveals only a small percentage devoted to news. The rest is either entertainment or advertising. Yet when mainstream newspapers run stories on supermarket tabs, they normally put them down for not being "real."

"Some of the mainstream press articles about the tabloids are quite kind, looking into the sociological relevance, the kind of people who write for them, or the fun, humorous side of this kind of news," said Sondra Lowell, who publishes a weekly roundup of tabloid tidbits. She also does a weekly radio spot on Los Angeles' KABC where she delivers, without snooty commentary, the essential news gathered from the supermarket tabloids.

"I stopped looking at the tabloids for trends and other points of significance when I realized that nobody cared that I had amassed this body of knowledge," she said. "I talked about it once on *CNN* and a couple of times on *National Public Radio*, but even the well-educated audiences [of those shows] did not recognize the necessity of keeping track of which dead presidents are still secretly alive and advising those running the country today." (Even former presidents who stay dead act as powerful talismans to current and would-be presidents.)

Most tabloid researchers recognize such recurring tabloid themes as "The Horatio Alger Story," "Government Waste" and "High Brought Low." Like urban myths, tabloid themes alter over time to reflect trends. For instance, stories about voices who speak from the dead are not much different than those featuring the late-1980s fad of "channeling." Various ways of predicting the future or of ensuring your child's success come and go, but the song remains the same.

The following categories roughly correspond to those noticed by others. Any differences in criteria are slight, although my analysis does occasionally differ from that of my predecessors.

Horatio Alger

The "Horatio Alger" theme stresses supposedly "old-fashioned" values. Its presence in tabs stems from at least 1968, when researcher Richard

Blaustein documented the theme in an unpublished paper in the Indiana University Folklore Archives at Bloomington, Indiana. The message encourages people to work, even if it does not bring them wealth. In the original Horatio Alger stories, the hard-working boy never received much more than a pat on the head from the boss or a small raise. The moral is not that hard work will bring you riches, but that it will satisfy the imperative to be good.

These stories speak to readers employed at dead-end, unglamorous jobs. A shopping mall janitor might read that one of his favorite TV characters, like Kramer on *Seinfeld*, was once a janitor, too. The connection lets him fantasize a way out of—even a reward for—his suffering. Like the tales of movie stars and starlets who are plucked out of mundane lives and groomed for luxury, the rags-to-riches stories provide the illusion of hope and fleeting comfort.

He goes from welfare to Major League baseball owner

Dennis Heindl was on welfare when he marched into a banker's office seeking a $70,000 loan. But first he demanded to know how much dough the bank had in its vaults!

Incredibly, Heindl got the loan — and today he's worth almost as much as the bank.

The 54-year-old go-getter owns a business that manufactures ball bearings and

RAGS TO RICHES

"When I sat in the Pirates' owner's box on Opening Day for the first time and

National Enquirer
8 April 1997

Since hard work rarely results in riches or fame, these stories are actually oppressive. They perpetuate the idea that a lifetime of service deserves recognition and rewards. Because this fantasy flies in the face of economic reality, such stories promote drudgery. The "Hard Work Pays" genre serves the status quo by providing false hope and the illusion of progress for people trapped in miserable lives. It's debatable whether the "stick to it" attitude should be adopted in what is, ultimately, a losing game.

High Brought Low

"High Brought Low" stories act as a foil for the potential excesses brought on by success. They stress the imperfections and failures of famous or powerful figures, caused by hubris or debauchery. Thus, articles describing Rock Hudson or Halston portray the men as deserving their AIDS-related deaths. Hudson, especially, was raked through the tabs. He seemed to have deliberately stepped off a clear path to fame and fortune and chose, instead, to become embroiled in homosexual promiscuity. It's no wonder his punishment was so swift, agonizing and even ignoble. This was nothing less than justice!

National Examiner, 20 May 1997

Fame and fortune are dangerous things in folklore and in tabloids. In late 1992, Oprah Winfrey was identified by the *National Enquirer* as having wrecked the marriage of her best friend by lavishing the newlyweds with too much money and other gifts. "She ruined our marriage with her generosity," the sad hubby said.

The same tragedy can befall "regular" people. Lottery winners are often destroyed, morally or financially, by their newfound, undeserved windfall: "$WEET REVENGE! $10 Million Lottery Winner Uses Every Penny to Get Even with His Enemies!" (*WWN*, 22 April 1997). Although the tabs hammer away at the themes of luck and fortune and the importance of believing in positive outcomes, they offer cautionary tales of those who forget humility and become greedy or arrogant.

The objects of a reader's envy are busted down a few pegs to show that in the end money and fame are worthless. Values such as honesty, loyalty and courage are the true measures of success. Even if the shopping mall janitor doesn't achieve success—as defined in the tabloids for "stars"—he can reassure himself that he's going to heaven. And in tabloids, there is most certainly an afterlife: "Iowa Farmer Sees the Faces of the Four Horses of the Apocalypse—& They're the Cartwrights!" (*Weekly World News*, 22 April 1997).

Courageous Crips

Courage is a guaranteed winner in the tabloid world. Brave dads (or dogs) are always dashing back into the flaming house to save the sleeping baby. Courage coupled with tenacity form perhaps the most admired combination. The stories that best represent these two traits fall into the "Courageous Crips" category. They are present in nearly every tabloid, in every issue. In a July 1994 issue of the *Globe*, a homeless and blind girl teaches herself to play the violin and ends up on her way to Harvard. Legless people, with their pluck and spunk, are forever clawing their way to the top of Mount McKinley, or simply dragging themselves to low-paying jobs for years on end—never losing their perky, optimistic views.

"Courageous Crip" stories might be inspirational, but more likely they predispose readers to false notions and unreasonable expectations of those in dire situations. On 22 April 1997 the *National Enquirer* reports on a car-wreck survivor: "47 STEPS TO TRIUMPH: Crippled Bride Wins 7-Year Battle to Walk Down the Aisle." Like the "Horatio Alger" stories, these stories are not based in reality. People with horrid diseases or handicaps face rough times and society tends to shun them.

GUTSY GAL WAITS TABLES — IN HER WHEELCHAIR

FIRST wheelchair waitress in America, Alycia Busciglio.

't
t
n
and carries
— in her

d only wheel-
l — but she

di-
for
ar-

an

)an Leahy,
espect for

t came in
clear she
' he says.
take

:areer
rking
kids.
ten a
out at

g other
le that
to live
a little
iays.

'There's no excuse anymore for handicapped people to sit around feeling sorry for themselves'

Weekly World News, 8 April 1997

Some advocates for the rights of handicapped people decry this coverage as being just as warped and dangerous to those suffering disabilities as politically correct euphemisms (such as "visually challenged" instead of "blind"). "Courageous Crip" stories carry an implicit message that those who do not face hardships stoically are failures. The crippled "heroes" seem to be distancing themselves from other cripples, implying that suffering is optional and that debility is a "state of mind." They are unrealistic role models for someone newly paralyzed in a car wreck or severely burned. For them, simply staying alive is often challenge enough.

What impact might these stories have on charity? Tabs lecture that money can be the cause of trouble, not relief. They've developed a sub-genre of stories depicting people who have faked their handicapped or destitute conditions. "Courageous Crip" stories allow non-crips the luxury of ignoring the needs of crippled people by giving the impression they "brought it on themselves" or are living in misery by choice.

The disability doesn't even need to be physical. Tabloids frequently report on homeless people who are secret millionaires. The *Examiner* once ran a story about a street person who won the lottery and gave all the money away, preferring not to deal with the "problems" he knew such money could cause.

Between August and October 1993, the *Weekly World News* ran several stories implying that beggars were, in reality, rich people or otherwise not deserving of charity—"Man Makes $275,000 as a Street

Beggar." The headline "Helping Others Can Wreck Your Life!" suggests that charity is bad for your health. On 22 April 1997, the *Sun* reports "Vagrant Woman's Filthy—and Filthy Rich!" A "bag lady," arrested for vagrancy in Atlantic City, N.J., is really an heiress worth $5 million. She dresses like a bum "for kicks."

A subset of these courage stories are tales of true generosity and charity—the "Mother Teresa" types. The charity displayed by a man who provides bicycles to poor children is always lauded in the tabs. The tabs are fond of setting up overnight charities to help a needy person or family and are well-known for their successes. In a 1987 interview in the *Fort Lauderdale News & Sun-Sentinel*, Generoso Pope, publisher of the *National Enquirer*, "admits he 'likes to reward people.' And that includes his readers. Ask him what he considers the *Enquirer*'s biggest coups and he makes no mention of 'exclusives' about Elizabeth Taylor or Sylvester Stallone. 'It's our money appeals for our readers,' Pope said. 'Our last one generated $250,000 for a burn victim who needed an operation.' " Stories of selfless behavior are valuable to readers and may inspire them to do good. As tab chronicler Sondra Lowell said, "Whenever I read stories [of generosity], I think, 'Why can't I be more like that?' "

Fatness Fetish

Fatness is an obsession with tabloids. It's fraught with implied moral failings. Anytime a celebrity gains or loses a few pounds it is newsworthy—particularly if the star is a woman. Women who lose pounds have typically done it through a "miracle" diet. Women who gain a few pounds are "blimping out" and described as if fighting a desperate battle of life and death. Even in death, obesity can be subtly mocked: "Woman's Corpse Was So-o-o Fat . . . 3 Angels Were Needed to Lift Her Soul into Heaven" (*Weekly World News*, 22 April 1997). Although the weighty dramas of Oprah and Liz are perennial favorites, tabs make room for newcomers like the popular TV hostess Rosie O'Donnell: "Tragic Family Secret Makes Rosie Balloon to 210 Pounds" (*National Enquirer*, 15 April 1997) and "Bette [Midler] to Rosie: LOSE WEIGHT OR DIE YOUNG" (*Globe*, 22 April 1997).

National Enquirer, 8 April 1997

Obese men pop up in tabs, too, but their fatness isn't portrayed tragically. "It's GUT-CHECK time for this rotund racer perched high on his hog. Steve Dumbleton has a weight problem—but don't feel sorry. The good-natured Australian biker plans on shedding the excess pounds and writing a how-to book for similar 'porkers'" (*Sun,* 22 April 1997).

Fatness as a gauge of moral or social value is a well-known tool of social control. Supporting an oppressive culture of beauty—with highly formalized standards—is the norm in supermarket tabs. A photo spread in the 22 April 1997 *Star* pours over the "failings" of stars caught without makeup or fancy attire while shopping, sitting at cafés or biking. Captions include "Goldie Hawn hides beneath a helmet and behind big sunglasses so you won't see her, uh, natural beauty," "Janet Jackson is practically unrecognizable here [wearing dumpy overalls], which is lucky for her," and "Mary Tyler Moore won't turn the world on with her smile with this washed-out look. How about a little lipstick, Mary?"

Should an actress accidentally flash a cellulite thigh she may very well find herself ridiculed on a "Gotcha!" page of photographs. At the '97 Oscars, a *Star* photographer snapped an unflattering shot of Jill Vendenberg's ample rear. (Vendenberg is the much younger and much taller girlfriend of Tony Curtis.) The caption reads, "What makes [her] think she can pull of this cheeky pantsuit? It reminds us of the *Saturday Night Live* skit of the refrigerator repairman with the low-slung pants." In the 22 April 1997 *National Enquirer,* Ivana Trump wins the Fashion

Victim of the Week award. "I-vana laugh out loud at Ivana!" Susan Baker writes. "Her lace and sequin dress is a horror show! It's so tight she looks like a stuffed sausage—and see-through sides are for desperate-to-work Tinsel Town starlets, not middle-aged moms."

Keeping Them in Their Place

Other tabloid stories stress that cheating and fraud will be met with punishment or shameful exposure. Tabloids love to run articles about bigamists, portraying the destitute wives of a polygamous man as victims of his immoral behavior. The stories suggest that were it not for the snake-like charms of the bigamist, these women would be financially well-off and happily married—tucked safe and sound within the folds of moral society. Their ostracism, though forgivable in this case, is caused by the morally demented bigamist.

The tabs' true "victims" of the bigamist are those who have lost their morals altogether and refuse to testify against their ex-husbands or who stupidly proclaim their continued love. As punishment, they are forced to stay on the periphery of good society. Those who decline to repent their unladylike ways are doomed to a village idiot status. Their loyalty, although admirable, is misplaced. The stories uphold the values of marriage and monogamy, but less obvious is the implication that women are prone to this sort of predator when they let their emotions run away. The unstated message is that women are vulnerable and need protection from unscrupulous men.

Women who don't know their place are shut up for years in cages, basements and attics. Men are allowed to control women with whatever force necessary. If a woman just cannot be made to obey, then the husband can get rid of her by losing her in a card game or trading her for a hunting dog. However, when women do seek revenge, they do it with flair: "Up . . . Up . . . and Away! Wife Chops Off Cheatin' Hubby's Penis—Then Sends It Aloft Tied to Balloons" (*Weekly World News*, 22 April 1997).

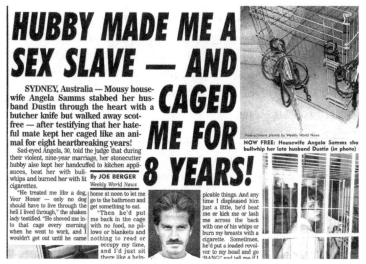

HUBBY MADE ME A SEX SLAVE — AND CAGED ME FOR 8 YEARS!

SYDNEY, Australia — Mousy housewife Angela Samms stabbed her husband Dustin through the heart with a butcher knife but walked away scot-free — after testifying that her hateful mate kept her caged like an animal for eight heartbreaking years!

Sad-eyed Angela, 30, told the judge that during their violent, nine-year marriage, her stonecutter hubby also kept her handcuffed to kitchen appliances, beat her with bullwhips and burned her with lit cigarettes.

By JOE BERGER
Weekly World News

"He treated me like a dog, Your Honor — only no dog should have to live through the hell I lived through," the shaken lady testified. "He shoved me into that cage every morning when he went to work, and I wouldn't get out until he came home at noon to let me go to the bathroom and get something to eat.

"Then he'd put me back in the cage with no food, no pillows or blankets and nothing to read or occupy my time, and I'd just sit there like a help-

picable things. And any time I displeased him just a little, he'd beat me or kick me or lash me across the back with one of his whips or burn my breasts with a cigarette. Sometimes, he'd put a loaded revolver to my head and go 'BANG!' and tell me if I

NOW FREE: Housewife Angela Samms sho bullwhip her late husband Dustin (in photo)

Weekly World News, 20 May 1997

Blacks are practically ignored by the tabloids, unless they fall into certain confined roles. For instance, a black man will be recognized if he has overcome a tremendous handicap to find a lower-echelon place in society. A blind and deaf black man is far more likely to show up in a tab story if he becomes a bicycle repairman than if he becomes a millionaire.

In 1982, an *Enquirer* editor was presented with the inspirational story of a young man who had survived a grain elevator explosion, suffered burns to 80% of his body, and went on to become a millionaire. This story fit perfectly with the tabloid's rags-to-riches motif, but then the editor asked if the man was black. When the reporter told him yes, the editor replied, "kill it," and returned to his work.

About the only time a tabloid will cover a black person is when he or she is doing something bizarre, such as when Michael Jackson slept with a pet chimpanzee, or committing a crime. There are no black people on the editorial staffs of any of the tabloids.

Societal "norms" are reinforced and reiterated in the tabs. Fascination with racial questions has been a staple of such publications from the very beginning, when even black-oriented tabloids reported on "mixed" couples.

UFOs

"Beware! . . . of Men in Black" cautions the *Sun* (22 April 1997). The sinister, black-clad men "appear to have one purpose in life . . . to dissuade UFO eyewitnesses from revealing any details of their experience." Nuclear physicist Dr. Franklin R. Ruehl writes that anyone with knowledge about UFOs might become victims of the "MIB"—subject to harassment, threats, interrogations, beatings and abductions. "Just who are these mysterious MIB?" Ruehl adds. "They may well be from a federal agency, such as the FBI, dispatched to help maintain the cloak of secrecy thrown over the UFO phenomenon by our government." To dissuade serious researchers, Ruehl says, "It is possible if you ever report sighting a UFO to the authorities . . . then the MIBs will be knocking at your door!"

Supermarket tabloids provide a convenient place to destroy certain political or scientific ideas while promoting the party line in conservative society. Many UFO researchers charge that tabloids are part of a deliberate scheme to deride and derail further study of unidentified flying objects or other paranormal phenomena.

Family claims 500-lb. space alien raided their refrigerator!

By BEATRICE DEXTER/*Weekly World News*

COLOGNE, Germany — A schoolteacher and his family ignited a media frenzy here when they revealed they had an encounter of the third kind — with an extremely fat space alien.

Horst Rottwenter, 52, his wife Lisa, 49, and son Walter, 19, swear they were accosted by the obese E.T. while spending a week in a country cabin near Cologne. The fat alien — who weighed an estimated 500 pounds and stood about 4 feet tall — materialized in the family's kitchen and demanded fried foods and pastries.

"It was this squishy silver-colored thing with tentacles ly rotund blob standing amid a pile of broken dishes.

The alien appeared to be unaware of their presence and went on searching the cupboards as they watched.

"We screamed in fear, but the creature didn't pay any attention," Rottwenter said. "It was single-minded. All it wanted to do was eat.

"When my wife called the police, they thought she was a prankster and never even sent anyone to investigate.

Weekly World News, 17 December 1996

The Moral Teachings of Tabs

While drug users are invariably "sickos" and degenerates, drinking alcohol is looked upon with favor. Not only will drinking beer help you live longer, lose weight and remove wrinkles, but by saving the cans you can build such useful items as canoes or cottages. Drunkenness produces hilarious situations, especially if one of the drinkers is fat and passes out on top of someone else, pinning him until help can arrive. And alcohol is always a fine reward for winning physical contests.

In 1983 the *National Enquirer* won the J. Edgar Hoover Memorial Award "for its efforts in the war against crime." It was the first time the American Federation of Police and American Police Hall of Fame had ever been presented the award to a newspaper. The federation praised the paper for exposing "[judges] who turn dangerous criminals loose with a slap on the wrist, parole boards that free violent convicts after they've served just a fraction of their sentences, and psychiatrists who free raving maniac killers to prey on society."

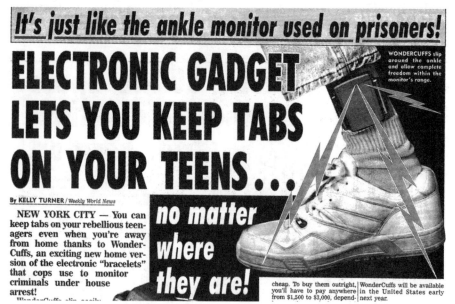

It's just like the ankle monitor used on prisoners!

ELECTRONIC GADGET LETS YOU KEEP TABS ON YOUR TEENS...

WONDERCUFFS slip around the ankle and allow complete freedom within the monitor's range.

no matter where they are!

By KELLY TURNER/*Weekly World News*

NEW YORK CITY — You can keep tabs on your rebellious teen-agers even when you're away from home thanks to Wonder-Cuffs, an exciting new home version of the electronic "bracelets" that cops use to monitor criminals under house arrest!

cheap. To buy them outright, you'll have to pay anywhere from $1,500 to $3,000, depend-

WonderCuffs will be available in the United States early next year.

Weekly World News, 20 May 1997

The *Enquirer* also offers a $10,000 reward to anyone who can help arrest any of the FBI's standing "Ten Most Wanted List."

Tabloid stories are full of moralistic stories designed to reinforce values that foster social control. In the tabloid world, hard work and honesty pay off and those who attempt to cheat their way through life will eventually be caught and punished. At times this "All-American" ethos is so strong it borders on hysterical xenophobia. Other stories stress the dangers of straying outside the limits of one's gender, class, or even race.

Despite their reckless and libelous image, tabloids never challenge the status quo. The only detectable variance from the establishment view is an occasional jab at government waste (chastising the funding of arcane science projects) or a trivial victory over the system (applauding an Average Joe who beat a traffic ticket). Of course, these defiant stories aren't threats to the party line and are just another form of reinforcement.

♦ ♦ ♦
4

Domestic Tranquility
How Tabs Support the Status Quo

In the long run only he will achieve basic results in influencing public opinion who is able to reduce problems to the simplest terms.
—Joseph Goebbels, 1942

As chapter 2 suggests, the use of supermarket tabloids as tools for espionage and the dissemination of propaganda seems exceedingly natural. Although they are widely read, they remain invisible to the mainstream media. In a time when subliminal advertising and the subtle effects of violence on TV warrant serious debate, tabloid content remains unexamined and ignored. Millions of people claim to never pick up a tabloid, yet they are exposed to the headlines as they pass through checkout counters. As outlined earlier, merely reading a headline has its effects.

Once again, the tabloids' anonymity is key. Even people who look for signs of media conspiracy to shape public opinion do not address tabloids. This publishing realm has the perfect camouflage—it's right in front of our noses.

In 1984 a reporter visited the offices of the *National Examiner* to try to expose its unethical practices. Editor Billy Burt allowed her full run of the office. She could speak to anyone at all and look at whatever she wanted as long as she didn't interfere with people doing their work.

On a hunch, she decided that a recent story about a boy born on a rollercoaster was a fake. She researched the story but could find no trace of it in any other newspaper. She called Burt on it, and he quickly told her that the story had been taken from a stringer in Brazil. She doggedly used the resources of her paper to try to track down the story, but came up with nothing. When she presented this to Burt he asked her to come into his office, where he shut the door.

"Look, I'll tell you a secret," he said in a sheepish tone. "That story's about 30 years old."

Aha! There was her answer. She couldn't find the incident because it was too old to show up on any of her databases. She swallowed Burt's ploy completely. A good reporter, she thought she had run her quarry to ground. There are few more gullible than a journalist.

The Not-so-Harmless Side of Tabs

Some of the tabloids' activities parallel those of *Reader's Digest*, which has been linked to the CIA. In 1988, *Covert Action Information Bulletin* no. 29 documented the magazine's connections to propaganda efforts, starting when copies of the *Digest* were air-dropped behind enemy lines during World War II. The article explains the links between the wholesome *Reader's Digest* and various American "psychological warfare" agents.

Like the *Digest*, tabloids are considered harmless. Nobody questions why tabloids and the *Digest* expend large sums of money on stories they never print, or which could have been written after making a few phone calls. Why *Reader's Digest*—a magazine supposedly devoted to reprints—would maintain a well-staffed Hong Kong office makes little sense. Its maintenance of other offices around the world is suspicious, especially its former Havana offices, which served as the focal point for its Central American editions.

In fact, the more innocuous the format, the more insidious the propaganda. *Reader's Digest* has the largest circulation of any publication in the world. It is pro-American and pro-Christian. Its editors and publishers are notoriously jingoistic. At one time American flag decals were dispensed to every employee. The *Digest* has been a useful outlet for disinformation, especially about the supposed Communist threat. Ronald Reagan even cited it as a source of information about the Sandinista government in Nicaragua! As if the man in charge of the Contras needed bolstering from reading material normally associated with musty dentist offices.

Tabloids—especially the *Enquirer*—spend tons of money on foreign stories, sending reporters all over the world for no discernible reason other than to gather information. They may claim to be looking for lost dinosaurs in the jungles of Zaire or for ancient astronauts in Peru. But none of these stories require on-the-ground reporting. Curiously, many of the sites are close to hard-to-monitor war zones or areas controlled by guerrilla movements.

The people who run and staff the tabs are anything but stupid. Many are former editors and reporters for the *Washington Post*, the *New York Times*, *Time* and *Newsweek*. American Media co-owner Michael Boylan is a former photo editor for the *New York Times*. Eddie Clontz, editor of the outrageous *Weekly World News*, used to be an articles editor at the Pulitzer-Prize-winning *St. Petersburg Times*.

Many tabloid reporters are bright, accomplished investigators and writers. Glen Troelstrup, who worked for the *National Examiner* for years, covered the Vietnam War for UPI and *Newsweek* before becoming an award-winning investigative reporter for the *Denver Post*. Tabloids also tend to hire the stereotypical transplanted Brit reporter, whose boorish and ruthless ways have become legend—*Lifestyles of the Rich and Famous* host Robin Leach got his start in America as an editor at the *Globe*.

Although pushy tabloid reporters are very effective at discovering well-kept secrets, they are often portrayed as too loutish to be involved in anything as subtle as politics. Still, it's interesting how often these guys pop up in curious places, from Monaco to Uganda. Being viewed as a lout might just provide the perfect cover. Like the old-time "house Negro" on Southern plantations, people will talk freely around them, believing them to be too dumb or too inconsequential to pose a problem. However, these reporters are famous for the lengths they will go to get a story. The use of disguises, fake credentials, bribes and other unwholesome methods of obtaining information are the same as those used by espionage agencies.

In mainstream politics the role of celebrity journalist is almost identical to that of politician. David Gergen rotates between stints as a Clinton aide to news "commentator" on PBS and network TV news shows. Michael Ledeen switches between jobs as a spy and conspirator for a secret foreign policy, to a news "commentator" for the *Wall Street Journal* and the conservative *Weekly Standard*, to a member of a "think tank" cranking out papers that will guide executive policy. Other celebrity journalist/politicians include Henry Kissinger, Dan Rather and William Safire. Certainly none of them would admit to associating with anyone connected with supermarket tabloids—even though they do.

Closer inspection of the people who own, write for and run the tabloids shows an astonishingly influential cast of characters. Les Aspin, the former mighty chairman of the Armed Forces committee, was once an *Enquirer* contributor. Rowland Evans and Robert Novak, of CNN's *Evans & Novak*, were once regular contributors to the *National Enquirer*. This is not something they list on their résumés anymore.

Jack Anderson, foe of Richard Nixon, has sold information to the *National Enquirer*. Like a politician admitting to a little marijuana smoking, Anderson now regrets his work for the *Enquirer*. Perhaps it was a youthful indiscretion. He needed the money. Yet Anderson maintains close ties to the same politicians, millionaires, and military and industry figures that associate with the owners and editors of the supermarket tabloids. One wonders what information a serious political journalist like Anderson could possibly have that would interest the *National Enquirer*. Anderson won't say.

Other movers and shakers are not so shy about their ties to the tabloids. When *Enquirer* founder Generoso Pope died in 1988, none other than former Secretary of Defense Melvin Laird gave the eulogy at the funeral. And why not? During the Vietnam War, Laird brought Pope to visit the White House, where he met with President Nixon and a group of grocery store chain executives. Until then, the southern supermarket chain Winn-Dixie had refused to carry the tabloid. After seeing the kind of clout Pope wielded, the paper was welcomed in every supermarket checkout line in the country.

Billy Graham, a regular at all the tabs as well as at many conservative mainstream dailies, is proud of his connection with the *National Enquirer*. In 1972 he told Reuters, "In my judgment, part of the success of the *National Enquirer* has been that there are millions of Americans who want clean, accurate reporting—but who like to see it in headlines. The *National Enquirer* has filled a vacuum. It also carries a number of religious-oriented stories," Graham said, confusing the word *religious* with *Christian*, "that I think have a tremendous appeal to people of all ages at this particular time of religious awakening in the country."

In 1985 Graham said, "Thanks to the *Enquirer*, I've been able to touch the lives of millions."

Billy Graham, while often portrayed as a buffoon, does seem to get around. He was the first preacher allowed to tour the Soviet Union, and he testified as a character witness at John Connally's trial for bribery in the 1970s.

Planting Stories

Estimates of the CIA's propaganda budget show it to be larger than the combined budgets of Reuters, United Press International, and the Associated Press. In *The CIA and the Cult of Intelligence*, Victor Marchetti and John Marks extrapolated approximate amounts of money and numbers of people devoted to propaganda. They determined that in the early 1970s at least 3,000 people were employed either on salary or on contract by the CIA to infiltrate and to influence media around the world. As economics Professor Sean Garvasi states in *Covert Action Information Bulletin*, the CIA may be considered the largest "news" organization in the world.

In 1977 Carl Bernstein reported in *Rolling Stone* that about 400 American media people were secretly working for the CIA. The same year, the *New York Times* practically bragged about the assistance it had given to the agency over the years, even naming editors and reporters who had participated.

According to a year-long *Penthouse* investigation, Copley Press was discovered to have at least 23 intelligence agents masquerading as reporters on its payroll. The company owns a number of newspapers in the United States and the worldwide Copley News Service, to which most supermarket tabloids subscribe.

Copley Press' relationship with intelligence agencies seems to have stemmed from a meeting between President Eisenhower and James S. Copley. Documents obtained by *Penthouse* confirm that Copley volunteered his news service to be "the eyes and ears" for the CIA and other "intelligence services." At subsequent meetings Ike directed Copley to provide U.S. agents with documents establishing suitable covers for American intelligence operatives. The relationship between the perennial money-losing "news organization" and the CIA continued into the 1980s. James Copley curried favor with the editors and publishers of right-wing (i.e., U.S.-sympathetic) newspapers, most notably with Agustin Edwards, publisher of the Chilean daily *El Mercurio*.

Copley News Service deployed agents around the world and even among American citizens. It released disinformation and other bogus news about perceived enemies, which were followed by incriminating editorials. Such tactics were used against the daughter of Daniel Ellsburg's attorney to imply that she was a Communist. The agency also planted editorials denouncing the Black Panthers.

The value of controlling the media, no matter how "trivial," is inestimable. In a world where a Johnny Carson joke about a supposed toilet paper shortage caused a real shortage during the oil embargo in the mid-1970s, no media forum is too inconsequential. As shown with Copley News Service, only a few of a company's employees need to be involved to have it function as an arm of an intelligence agency. Such an arrangement can be made from the top down, thus limiting the number of people with explicit knowledge of ties to the CIA or to any other outside organization.

Both the CIA and the Soviet KGB (and their subsidiary intelligence agencies) have accused and exposed each other of "planting" various stories in the foreign press to influence the masses. In the early 1990s, stories of American baby brokers stealing or purchasing children of impoverished Central American people were blamed on old Soviet propaganda. In 1989 I wrote a bogus story for the *National Examiner* in which children at a South American "organ farm" were forced to work as field hands until it was time to part them out.

Weekly World News, 20 May 1977

Dishwasher executed — for peeing on Fidel Castro's dinner!

HAVANA — Justice was swift and deadly for Alfredo Castaneda, a dishwasher in the palace of Fidel Castro, after he was caught urinating on the Cuban dictator's food.

"A kitchen supervisor walked in and found the man defiling El Jefe's (The Boss's) hamburger dinner," a palace spokesman said.

"The culprit immediately ran from the kitchen through a rear door and escaped out the back."

When informed of the stomach-turning prank, an outraged Castro sent troops to search for Castaneda.

Less than an hour later, a soldier spotted the 30-year-old man on a street two miles from the palace and put three bullets into his brain.

"The young soldier will no doubt receive a medal for his heroic service to El Jefe," the palace spokesman said.

PEEVED DICTATOR: Castro sent troops after the man who urinated on his hamburger dinner.

In 1985 the CIA was discovered to have published and distributed to villagers throughout Sandinista-controlled Nicaragua a booklet on how to commit industrial sabotage and attack police stations. During the Cold War, South America and Africa were constant battlegrounds between rival superpower spy agencies for the "hearts and minds" of the people who lived there.

In the late 1980s and early 1990s, law enforcement agencies in this country were accused of fomenting bogus "satanic" crime waves or spates of mass child abuse, which resulted in widespread fear and horrendously damaging prosecutions. Whether the media is actively complicit or not, it certainly makes such deceptions easier. Police officers say they believe Satanists are at work, the news media hypes it, and soon the public perceives a problem without any evidence. If the deception is successful enough in cowing the public, people may begin to tolerate certain abuses of their rights to stave off the manufactured menace. Controlling mass media can mean the ability to shape public opinion, especially when these opinions are reinforced by "polls" undertaken by the same media outlets that use the results to bolster further "news" stories.

Tabloid stories, in their bipolar world of darkness and light, are often home to stories that help demonize establishment foes. Fidel Castro, Ayatollah Khomeini, the Soviets, Saddam Hussein, along with gays and blacks have all been cast at one time as fearsome agents of the devil. The forces of good are just as clear-cut. Police may stumble from time to time and politicians may introduce pork barrel legislation, but they are never truly corrupt. U.S. military boys are always portrayed as knights in shining armor. Troops stationed in Saudi Arabia were even blessed with visitations by Elvis and Jesus Christ.

Reporting and Spying Techniques

Tab reporting methods borrow techniques used by intelligence agencies to gather information and have almost nothing in common with what is thought of as modern journalism. Tab reporters do not depend on press releases or PR people to give them stories. Instead, they are sent out to collect as much information as possible, which they hand to editors who "control" them. All information is sourced, dated and filed in libraries staffed by researchers and tape transcribers. Planting moles and using decoys, hidden cameras and surveillance are the norm for tabloid reporting. So, too, is the practice of paying for information. Like spies, tab reporters know that once people accept money, they are linked to you, giving you leverage should they ever want to keep the relationship secret. Speaking of the company's flagship publication, Tony Fromt, vice president of Globe Communications, said, "*Globe* is one of the major practitioners of checkbook journalism in America and we make no apologies. We'll do anything to get a jump on our rivals, provided it's within the law."

Mainstream articles about tabloids never fail to mention the lengths to which their reporters and photographers will go to get a story or a picture. Photographers will helicopter over people's homes and use enormous long-range lenses and infrared filters to catch people who thought they had privacy. Tab reporters will buy airplane seats near their quarry just to eavesdrop on conversations. Sometimes they stage car "accidents," ramming someone's car to get a word with that person. Tabloid reporters routinely impersonate priests, bellboys, long-lost relatives—anyone to get a story.

The stakeout is matched only by those done by detectives. Tab photographers will spend a week in underbrush outside the Betty Ford Clinic to get a shot of Liz Taylor. If the situation calls for more intensive or long-term surveillance, tab reporters are dispatched in teams to cover all points of entry and exit. The house next door is likely to become a field headquarters for the stakeout team, which communicates with tiny walkie-talkies, listens through walls with parabolic microphones, and tails people with three or more cars to avoid detection. Tab reporters have hidden in dumpsters, disguised themselves as llamas, and broken into countless houses to get close to their prey.

On an assignment for the *Globe* in the early '90s, I rented a limousine and driver along with a van. After driving up from Seattle, I practically lived in the parking lot of the Vancouver airport for five days waiting for one of Sharon Stone's boyfriends to show up. My job? To tell him Sharon had sent me and to get him into the limo. There were at least two other people watching his movements in the airport, two more people inside the airline, and another two tailing him in L.A. All of us were just waiting for him to go home so we could confirm that he knew Sharon Stone.

When I got him in the car, he got skittish and foolishly took out his cellular phone and called his voice mail. As I was recording everything with a tape recorder, I also captured his "secret" access code as he punched it in. Even when he realized something was wrong, he continued to give away information about himself, his relationship with

Sharon Stone, and other parts of his personal life. Within five minutes of dropping him off at a hotel lobby to meet a woman there, all of these details were transmitted to an editor in Los Angeles.

Needless to say, this kind of spying is practiced really one other place.

◆ ◆ ◆

5

Propaganda at the Checkout Stand

One thing that makes discussion of American "supermarket tabloids" difficult is the widespread belief among self-titled intellectuals that they already know everything about them. In a whopping case of hubris, people who readily (even haughtily) admit they never read tabloids are perfectly comfortable saying they know what's in them.

It is no longer a question for establishment media of whether supermarket tabloids exert influence over mainstream news outlets. They may try to ghettoize these weeklies by deriding their supposedly unethical reporting tactics or simply denying their existence, but by 1997, political events have forced the mainstream to recognize supermarket tabs can and do shape the way other news outlets present or report "news."

What remains a question for the establishment is the impact these papers have on the public mind and their influence over politics at every level. Supermarket tabloids don't usually cover presidential races because they are not very exciting. Tabs want to interest their readers with scandalous and bizarre behavior. The main nexus between politics and tabloid coverage occurs when public figures do something tawdry.

Certainly the supermarket tabs have proven themselves quite capable of drastically changing things at a presidential level. In 1987, the

National Enquirer sealed Gary Hart's fate with a snapshot of the presidential candidate on a booze & cruise trip with Donna Rice. In 1994 the *Globe* was the first to publish the name of the alleged rape victim in the infamous Kennedy-Smith rape trial. This was immediately aped by both the *New York Times* and NBC television. Both went out of their way to deny the tabloid had anything to do with it. Although 5 million people had already learned the woman's name and seen her picture, these mainstream pundits acted, literally, as if the tabloids didn't exist.

While running for president in 1992, Bill Clinton was nearly felled by Gennifer Flower's sex-confessions revealed in the *Star*. Certainly the raucous press conference she gave (*Star* was not about to let the mainstream co-opt this one) set a new standard for such forums. Reporters shouting questions about the size of Clinton's penis are not a lot different than reporters shouting at the president to confirm or deny that he really "ate pussy like a champ!"

Politicians may pretend to hate this sort of "decline" in press relations and claim they'd rather talk about "issues," but when given an opportunity to do just that, they are best known for their sound-bite slogans and ad hominem attacks.

As *National Enquirer* editor Iain Calder has explained many times, his paper published the 1987 Gary Hart "Monkey Business" photos only because the *Miami Herald* had already created a sensation with their botched stakeout of Hart's apartment. Had it not been for that, Calder doubts any *Enquirer* readers would have cared. The *Enquirer* then ruthlessly finished the job for the *Herald*, and its photos were duly reproduced on the front pages of mainstream newspapers across the land—along with high-minded snorts about "shoddy journalism."

Tabs report on sensational aspects of the presidential races and the mainstream papers ape their lurid coverage, adding prissy apologies. After all, it is only a duty to set the record straight that "makes good newspapers wince and publish," wrote Joann Byrd of the *Washington Post*, on 16 August 1992, in defending her paper's coverage of the *Star*'s coverage of Gennifer Flowers.

The 1992 presidential campaign's most sensational story was the *Star's* revelations about Bill Clinton's extramarital affairs. The story nearly proved politically fatal to Clinton, and it set the agenda for press coverage of him for years. For weeks the mainstream press jabbered on about it. The *Star's* story initiated an open season on Bill Clinton and any other candidate to probe their sexual histories. Even President Bush started getting asked if he'd ever cheated on his wife. Pundits on talking-head shows and writers of op-ed pieces stroked their chins about whether they should even be discussing the topic—all the while noting that none of the candidates would say yes or no to the adultery question.

The *Star's* coverage of Flowers did more than spawn clones in the mainstream media. Other media outlets explored the much murkier story of George Bush's supposed paramour, Jennifer Fitzgerald (the "other Jennifer," as Hillary Clinton put it). "Good" newspapers like the *Washington Post* hinted that it was common knowledge to newsroom cognoscenti, but they just couldn't pin the story down. They could neither confirm nor deny the column inches of rumor they published.

Meanwhile, the *Enquirer* defended Bush as a loyal husband.

During the '96 presidential campaign, when *Time* and *Newsweek* were hawking cover stories about Dick Morris, the mighty and crafty political adviser, the *Star* was poised to take him down. And when the paper did, it happened fast.

The *Star's* explosive story of then-married Morris and his $200-an-hour prostitute girlfriend could have had enormous impact on the election, especially since Morris had guided Clinton's outlook and vision closer to that of moderate, socially conservative Americans. However, the *Star* was hampered by its weekly publishing schedule. Its next issue wouldn't be on the stands until September 2. The editors decided to feed the story to the *New York Post*, so they would be sure to get proper credit for the scoop. The *Post* ran the story of Morris on August 29—the day Clinton was scheduled to deliver his acceptance speech at the Democratic Convention. The papers had called Morris the day before, so he knew it was coming; he knew the *Star* had a video of the couple in bathrobes, standing on a balcony at the Jefferson Hotel in Washington, D.C.

Morris resigned the day the paper hit the stands saying, "I will not subject my wife, family or friends to the sadistic vitriol of yellow journalism. I will not dignify such journal ism with a reply or an answer, and I never will."

The *New York Times* printed the story the next day. And on September 2, *Star* readers got the whole lurid story of the high-priced hooker, her intimate diary, and lots of details of their months-long affiar (for which she dropped other clients to accommodate him). Of course, there were big color pictures and tantalizing details of how he would purposely call Clinton, just to show off his power.

Even when feeding off the tabs, establishment news likes to pretend the supermarket tabloids don't exert any influence over its decisions. When NBC reporters wanted to reveal the name of the alleged rape victim at the Kennedy's Palm Beach estate, they used the excuse that the woman's name was well-known within Palm Beach society, not because her name and photo had already been published in the *Globe*.

When Ted Koppel wanted to rhapsodize on the ethics of revealing rape victims' names, *Nightline* acknowledged the tabloid's existence but illustrated the *Globe* by holding a copy of the *Enquirer*. Koppel then solicited the opinions of *NBC News* president Michael Gartner, who made damn sure nobody thought he would ever take the *Globe* into consideration when it came to a decision of such journalistic moment.

"Well, we didn't do it because the *Globe* had done it, Ted," Gartner reassured us. "The woman's name had become quite well-known in the Palm Beach community."

With these words Gartner spilled the elitist beans. The knowledge of the bejeweled matrons of Palm Beach meant more to him than the 5 million people across the country who had read the woman's name and had seen her picture in the *Globe* that week. From then on in the show, the *Globe* became the Newspaper with No Name—referred to only as "the tabloid." Nobody from ABC or any of the network news programs asked a representative from Globe Communications to come onto their hallowed shows. When *Globe* editor Wendy Henry pointed out to AP reporters that there was no crime in being a rape victim, her philosophy was assumed to be a flimsy cover for her gross sensationalism.

The tabs' emphasis on the sensational should not suggest there is no political ideology at work when choosing and writing stories—there most definitely is. Unfortunately for all politicians, it is anti-politics. Perhaps this is why Ross Perot was not attacked by the tabs in '92; why he was pictured waterskiing while his opponents strangled in their ties. After Perot dropped out, *Weekly World News* columnist Ed Anger said he had "no choice" but to vote for Bush. Even if Bush were a "stark raving maniac" he would still have to vote for him—because he's not a lawyer!

Our America and Ed Anger's America

Of all the overtly political content in supermarket tabloids, the rantings of *Weekly World News*' Ed Anger in his "My America" column are the most noticeable and right-wing. His frothing and frenetic screeds against homosexuals, molly-coddled prisoners, uppity women and presumptuous foreigners are a caricature of a redneck more brutal than Archie Bunker.

Weekly World News
20 May 1997

Like the corporate creation of Betty Crocker, there is no Ed Anger. Ed Anger, a sputtering Korean War vet with a metal plate in his head, was invented by a skinny Jewish guy named Rafe Klinger in 1981. Ed's idiotic ravings caught on and became a staple in the paper. No issue of the *News* would be complete without one of Ed's tirades about some trend that has made him "pig-biting mad."

Since Klinger's firing in 1988, Ed now belongs to *WWN*, despite Klinger's attempts in court to claim ownership. Klinger's creature finds a receptive audience at *WWN* for a variety of reasons. His ridiculous twist on reality produces ready-made humor for morning disc jockeys around the country. Little fan clubs in his honor have sprung up in the most liberal of locales. Ed is camp.

At first no one knew just how to take him. His Cro-Magnon view so closely parallels many Americans' real opinions that many thought Ed was real. Letters supporting and condemning his views arrived at the office. Clearly, a lot of people took him seriously. This suggests the "hidden" politics of both the tabloids and their readers are a tad on the conservative side. Further examination of tabloid content bears this out.

Xenophobia and the Gulf War

All the tabloids show a bias against non-Christians and foreigners. From a political viewpoint, this xenophobia is inherently reactionary. Current rulers value "anti-outsider" press, as illustrated by the tabloids' hearty stoking of the flames of war during Operation Desert Storm.

British tabloids did the same thing. The *Sun* headlined a story "Iraqi Pig Rapes BA Girl." The more "respectable" *Daily Mirror* fomented hatred with its article "Grinning Soldier Rapes Jet Girl at Gunpoint." The *Star* titled a story "Iraqi Animals on Rampage," while the *Express* told of "hundreds of Britons dragged screaming from buses and taxis at gunpoint." When Jordan's King Hussein expressed reluctance to go along with the destruction of Iraq, *Sun* headlines declared, "We Don't Want You, King Rat!" *Today* published details of Saddam's "blood-stained war machine."

These editions in Great Britain appeared within a couple of weeks of Iraq's invasion of Kuwait on 1 August 1990, during which fewer than 200 people were killed. The papers thought it crucial to begin pumping up the war fever right away. The tabloids keep a constant, low-level fire going under the feet of any would-be challengers to the status quo.

Jesus appears to our boys in Saudi

DAZZLING SUNSET VISION STUNS TROOPS

Sun, 19 March 1997

George Bush recognized the power of supermarket tabloids. "I am especially grateful for the support of all at Globe Communications for our efforts in the Persian Gulf," Bush wrote to editorial director Phil Bunton, who presided over all three of Globe's tabloids. "It's important that our courageous troops face this historic challenge knowing that they have the support of millions of people around the world."

Indeed, he should have been grateful. The supermarket tabs pack a propaganda punch unmatched by any other news outlet. With a tradition of anti-Arab bias and jingoistic élan, these papers were well-prepared to help out when Bush needed a devil. Before and during the war, the *Globe* festooned its cover with yellow ribbons, American flags and exhortations to "Support America's Heroes." This fit very well with the image *Globe* tries to project—hard-working, honest and clean.

The *Sun* (better known for its stories of dog-babies and toilet paper diets) did its part with a deft change in an already-scheduled story about AIDS-infected hookers sent to the U.S. by the evil masters of Iran. By the time the story hit the stands, the prostitutes came from Iraq. The *Sun* concocted a string of anti-Saddam stories, though they seemed to lack editorial consistency: One week Saddam was receiving battle plans from an undead Adolf Hitler, the next he was dying of brain cancer. One issue revealed his secret hideout in the Alps, while another revealed a fortress deep in the Rockies. In a single issue, the *Sun* accused Saddam of being both a homosexual *and* a swinish gigolo.

The normally humdrum *National Examiner* must have pleased the Bush folks the most. The *Examiner's* atrocity stories rivaled German baby-eater stories of World War I for both grotesqueness and mendacity. Like all modern legends, they passed into the public subconscious without much scrutiny.

One *Examiner* cover featured a Massachusetts housewife, Valentine Swinson, hiding her face while confessing, "I Was Raped and Tortured by Saddam." Inside, her lurid interview described how Saddam lectured her about submitting to "Allah's greater glory" before having her gang-raped by the Iraqi high command. In case readers might think it heartless to exploit a rape victim's pain, the paper claimed that a "fee paid to Valentine Swinson by the *Examiner* for her cooperation has been donated to an international charity."

Another issue claimed Saddam tortured and killed household pets, illustrating the story with a photo of Saddam strangling a plump Siamese cat. The *Examiner* claimed to have found a former classmate who remembered Saddam's fondness for dog stew, which he prepared by hacking the dog to pieces and throwing it into a pot—hair and all.

Of course, there was no Valentine Swinson (the woman in the photos was a low-paid photo assistant), and tab readers are notoriously fond of their pets. Dog-eating is a vulgarity normally reserved for maligning Asian refugees who move into the neighborhood. But this was war and all was fair.

None of the other stories were real either. But so what? They were no less real than some of the bogus stories invented by the U.S. government, which mainstream media dutifully transmitted, such as the one that claimed Iraqi soldiers ripped premature babies from incubators in Kuwaiti hospitals. Nothing in the tabs conflicted with what was already "known" about Saddam and Iraq. The tabs simply provided more lurid stories and made the mainstream's lies more believable, strengthening and validating the war hysteria. This hysteria, in turn, enabled the military to cause much real-life suffering and misery without public outcry or scrutiny.

Vilifying David Koresh

The siege and subsequent mass death at Mount Carmel in Waco, Texas, in the early spring of 1993 provides another means to test the tabloids' willingness to challenge the party line. The Branch Davidians were charismatic Christians—a group thought to be part of tabloids' readership. They burned to death as government tanks pushed burning wreckage into a fiery heap. Just as the *Examiner* had taken a risk by maligning Jim Bakker while he was on trial in 1989, the tabloids had to make a decision as to how to cover this story. Should they side with government or with their Christian readership? In this case, they chose the establishment line.

Of all the stories that appeared in the six supermarket tabloids, only one slightly questioned the government's excuse, that David Koresh was a madman and should take the blame for all the suffering. A year after the tragedy, an article in the *Examiner* claimed "government insiders" linked Waco and the mass suicide in Jonestown, Guyana. The article stated that more than 1,000 Americans were victims of CIA mind-control experiments gone horribly wrong. It noted the eerie similarities between the two events and suggested that the followers of both "crazed charismatic leaders" were "enslaved" by these mind-control experiments. Also, bullet wounds found in corpses at both places suggested some were assassinated and did not commit suicide.

The remainder of the tabloid coverage of the event was decidedly pro-government.

4 May 1993 *Examiner*
Describes Koresh's crazed plot to return from the dead and states, "Mad messiah burned his own kids to a crisp so he'd live again." The explosive story inside.

4 May 1993 *Enquirer*
News team brings readers the story of "suicide horror" as Waco survivors reveal what really happened in the final hours. "Mommy, am I going to die?" In those frightful final hours Koresh ordered one man mercilessly gunned down when he tried to escape. The team also discovered that Koresh had "lured youngsters to deaths with toys," enticing them into the flames.

11 May 1993 *Enquirer*

Offers an explanation as to why Koresh would have deliberately set about his own destruction in a story headlined "Mad Messiah Needed a Miracle to Keep a Reign on Doubting Disciples." The same story, however, reveals that the coroner who examined the corpses was an "incompetent butcher" who had botched autopsies repeatedly in the past.

11 May 1993 *Enquirer*

"Waco Cult Vows Vengeance" and "FBI Beefs Up Probe as Fanatics Go Underground" help keep the story alive for future use. Notice how Koresh has already been slated for a return from the dead in preceding stories. In the tabloid world, as we all know, it's difficult for a top-seller to really die.

11 May 1993 *Star*

"Gospel of Hate"—Read for the first time mad messiah David Koresh's twisted message. The Star *also ran a story about "Hell's little angel," a silent waif who lost everything in the fire (meaning her parents) and is so traumatized she has become mute. "Now she must even learn to speak again."*

18 May 1993 *National Examiner*

Holds out the hope that Koresh might still be alive. An eyewitness reports that the "Waco whaco" had crawled out through a secret tunnel.

18 May 1993 *Globe*

"First Look Inside the Sex-Crazed Cult's Compound." Of course, no such "look" was possible since the entire complex was destroyed by fire and explosions. Nevertheless, the story describes how Koresh "gorged on sex and specially prepared meals and slumbered on a luxurious queen-sized bed with sumptuous satin sheets in a private room above the infamous bunker where he kept his mighty arsenal." (It is ludicrous to describe the Branch Davidians' collection of semiautomatic rifles as "mighty"—especially when compared to the Blackhawk helicopters and 100-man SWAT teams that attacked their church.)

18 May 1993 *Sun*

Satan's face in Koresh's suicide inferno. The same story appeared a week earlier in the Weekly World News, *yet the stories were done independently.* WWN's *shorter lead time let it hit the stands ahead of the* Sun, *thus "scooping" the competition. The photograph for the* Sun *was credited to an amateur photographer who was lucky to capture the astonishing image. (Satan in all his digitized malignancy also appeared in the smoke above the L.A. riots and in the fires of Kuwait.)*

25 May 1993 *Sun*

Reports there's a supposed Koresh treasure buried somewhere in Texas— probably near Corpus Christi, whose name means "body of Christ." Self- proclaimed "expert" Donald Horn gives the account and claims to be working on finding the fortune by consulting "clues" hidden in the Bible.

25 May 1993 *Globe*

"Paintings of Pain: Koresh's Kids' Death Drawings Bear Cult's Chilling Secret—Nightmare of Sick Sex and Violence." (The drawings by the sur- viving children from Mount Carmel mainly portray helicopter gunships firing down on their heads.)

29 June 1993 *Star*

"Waco Madman's Crazy Plot to Kill Madonna" manages to squash two proven sellers into the same headline. Police say they are worried that any surviving followers of the "maniacal cult-leader" would "still carry out his evil orders." Why? Because Koresh supposedly wanted the pop star to "join his harem." (Koresh was never known to have had a harem.)

6 July 1993 *Globe*

"Double Trouble"—a dead ringer for Koresh is dogged by his unfortunate similarity. "People think Koresh survived the fire and I'm him," fumes a 23- year-old cable TV installer.

29 June 1993 *Globe*

"Resurrection!" Koresh's granny wants to dig him up. Koresh is called the "maniac messiah."

7 September 1993 *Globe*

"Koresh Picked Me to Be His Bride When I Was Only Ten"—a girl's amazing story of escape from the clutches of the Waco Madman—another milking of the Koresh-as-sex maniac theme.

Government Secrets and UFOs

With UFO coverage, tabloids appear to depart from the government's line. They do not seem to accept government claims that there are no UFOs. Tabs often print stories of UFO sightings, cow mutilations and crop circles: "EXPERTS CONFIRM: 1997 Photo of UFOs Taken by Astronaut Is REAL" (*Weekly World News*, 22 April 1997). They even run stories of UFO researchers thwarted by an extremely secretive intelligence community (foreshadowing *X-Files* by many years) that refuses to release any information on the subject beyond their denials.

The *Enquirer* does not offer rewards to people who can ferret out compelling evidence of what the government is hiding. It restricts itself to challenging readers to bring in irrefutable proof of alien visitations—such as an intergalactic spacecraft or even a Martian in the flesh! Tabloids are not at variance with the government, since UFOs are not necessarily craft from other worlds. They do not address the UFO community's main beef with the government, which is that officials refuse to release information already obtained by the Air Force and other agencies. A reward for bringing in ET alive is not a challenge to the status quo.

"War" on Drugs

Tabloids prefer to keep to the government line even when a perfectly good sensational story could question the government's policies. In the spring of 1990 I was assigned a story about two drug offenders given life sentences at hard labor in the Georgia prison system for possession of small amounts of cocaine. They had received the sentences under an almost forgotten law dredged up by the prosecutor.

My editor, Lee Harrison, wanted the slant to be "Finally, Justice Comes to Druggies," despite the obvious potential for an injustice to have occurred. When I called the parties involved I found that the statute was liable to be overturned on appeal, that the defense attorneys planned to fight it, and that even the judge considered the sentence unduly harsh. There was no justice at all.

Miscarriage of justice is not enough to interest the tabloid reader, so I suggested the "Little Guy Getting Screwed by the Government" angle. Instead, why not do a story titled "Hard-Hearted Prosecutor Uses Archaic Law to Send Men to a Chain Gang—for Life!" Since I was sure I could get good quotes from even the judge's office, I thought the story could fly.

Harrison refused. He insisted that readers wanted to hear about "druggies" receiving draconian punishments and that's what they were going to get. My arguments that this kind of story would only perpetuate harm were useless. My arguments that Harrison, as an occasional drug user, was being hypocritical were useless. "It doesn't matter if I take drugs," he said. "The reader wants to hear how the guy got life! Just do the story!"

"But I can give you just as sensational a story from the defendants' points of view—I mean even the judge is pissed off . . ."

"Just do the story like it says on the lead sheet, mate."

I let the story languish on my desk and refused to do it, pissing off my boss and perhaps jeopardizing my job. Since Phil Brennan, another reporter, refused to do any stories contrary to his Catholic beliefs, I felt I had some grounds to refuse it. The story was reassigned, ironically, to Brennan.

This anecdote illustrates the unbending desire to both feed the readership its perceived wants and to follow the establishment line, even when the editors were opposed to what they were doing. Hypocrisy wasn't enough to shame them, and the potential bad effects their stories may have on society were just as meaningless. Whether this reflects a "bottom-line" mentality that cannot risk losing a single reader or an insidious adhesion to the party line is impossible to tell.

What Tabs Say About O.J.

The press coverage of the O.J. Simpson criminal trial is an example of tabloid reporting at its best. In the beginning, establishment papers copped their usual indignant pose and claimed there was nothing worth reading in the tabs. They tried to rhapsodize about ethical considerations, devoting themselves to stories or shows discussing whether or not they should even be discussing the trial.

Meanwhile the public stampeded for news in tabs, news they could find faster and in more detail than anything the mainstream had to offer. Sales of tabloids jumped 30%. Soon enough tab readers got a gander at the 15-inch knife O.J. was said to have bought; they got inside information from O.J.'s cook and from Nicole Simpson's therapist. Scooped so badly, the mainstream made charges of "checkbook journalism," hauling out media guru Ben Bagdikian to pronounce that payments to sources, were it to become widespread, would cause "the whole process of reporting [to] be distorted."

The clerks who sold O.J. the fearsome-looking knife were attacked for selling their story to the *Enquirer* for $12,500, but even prosecutor Marcia Clark had to admit, "These people were telling the truth; they're being asked to tell what happened. That's no more nor less that what they're being asked to do in court for free."

Establishment commentators pretended to be sickened and shocked by the thought of a news agency paying for its raw materials. Former federal prosecutor Jeff Toobin wrote in a *New Yorker* article "Cash for Trash" that paying witnesses would unduly influence them to say whatever they were told to. He states, "Witnesses who take money from tabloids automatically raise questions about their credibility" and referred to the practice as "buying witnesses." He spat at lawyers who profited from setting up interviews as the "cash for trash" bar.

He fretted about guilty people going free because of "settlements" made, wildly speculating that Michael Jackson was a "serial pedophile" about to "escape punishment" when negotiations (which involved O.J.'s criminal defense lawyer Johnny Cochran) seemed to halt the investigation into a supposed child-molestation charge.

Not only did Toobin forget about innocent until proven guilty (and Jackson was never even charged!), he conveniently forgets that paid informants are the stock and trade of prosecutors everywhere. Without even considering the pressure put on a prosecution witness to either testify or go to prison, Toobin is oblivious to the reverse of his claim: If a cash payment to a defense witness is so damning, why isn't it for the prosecution? If cash for a newspaper story, not testimony, shows craven motivation, what prosecutor could hope to win when nearly every witness called by the state is also paid by the state for his or her testimony?

In the end, even the mainstream had to admit that the tabloids' stories on O.J. scooped them every time, were more detailed, and were more accurate. They ended up conceding this one and stopped trying to outdo the tabs, whose sources were nearly always better anyway. As "quickie" paperbacks hit the stands within weeks of damn near anything that happened during the investigation and trial, the mainstream gritted its teeth and duly reported what they'd heard in court that day: that this or that tabloid publication was to be banned for prospective jurors, which just gave the tabs free advertising.

Newsday predicted in early July '94 that the free-market frenzy of O.J. stories would soon collapse, but three months later the O.J. story had appeared on the cover of *Globe* for the 16th week in a row. And the *Globe* was still budgeting a minimum of $20,000 a week to cover the story in an almost meticulous way. The only tab to take a firm position on O.J.'s innocence, the paper offered a million dollars to anyone who could prove O.J.'s innocence. The offer drew a couple of hundred thousand responses, which produced a few dozen leads and, in the end, a story or two.

In contrast to would-be reporters like Jeff Toobin, many reporters at the *Globe* saw a "lot of shadows" in this case. Long-time investigative reporter Ken Harrell (who had once gone undercover to get a story on the Ku Klux Klan) was going to stand by the defendant's innocence until O.J. was proven guilty beyond a doubt. Since Harrell's job was to gather facts and report them, he was in one of the better positions to make a judgment.

If O.J. had been found guilty in the initial trial, however, Harrell said he would have started writing stories about O.J. in prison. Before the civil trial, Harrell wrote about the acquitted man putting his life back together.

♦ ♦ ♦

6

Tab Readers
They Don't Move Their Lips When They Read

"America is a 300-pound woman. This woman has two dogs, two TVs, hypochondria, and no secondary education. She's also broke, bored to tears, over 40 (her husband was once alcoholic, unfaithful, crippled or laid off), and yet, despite all, she believes in life after death. Got to be. She's the only person who'd buy the *Enquirer*," claims D. Keith Mano, snooty pundit of the *National Review*.

Mano's attitude sums up what a lot of the "intelligentsia" think of people who buy tabloids. If this disparaging caricature were correct, then Mano assumes that at least 11 million people in our country fit this description. Mano's editor at the *National Review* once called the *National Enquirer* "a disgrace to journalism." Even filmmaker John Waters, no social gem himself, said, "I'm convinced that the typical *Enquirer* readers move their lips when they read, are physically unattractive, badly dressed, lonely and overweight. Especially overweight."

The truth is few people know just who reads the tabloids. Tab editors, who have access to market studies and focus groups, say they'd rather rely on their gut instincts and on the deluge of letters received each week to guide them to their audience. Nevertheless, data collected primarily by advertising agencies gives us glimpses of what tabloid readers are like. These surveys indicate that tabloid readers are strikingly normal, which may be too painful for the snoots to consider.

Tabloid readers are generally middle- to lower-class whites. They work at blue- and pink-collar jobs. A little more than half own pulsating shower heads; their favorite meals are steak, chicken and lobster (in that order); and the majority own outdoor grills. Not exactly bizarre. A lot like everyone else, really.

One study commissioned by the *Star* in 1985 revealed that 30% of its readers had a home computer. Yet in 1984, home computer ownership for the entire country was just 8%. This, along with other information, suggests tabloid readers are far from stupid. An oft-cited 1984 Roper poll showed 20% of tabloid readers used the word *accurate* to describe the tabs. This is supposed to be a shocking statistic illustrating how such people must be half-wits. It also shows that 80% of the respondents questioned what they read. Could the mainstream press boast such independent-minded thinkers in their readership?

Contrary to the mainstream image, most tab readers are not embarrassed to buy or be seen reading their tabloids. They seem skeptical of some of the stories, but regard tabs as legitimate sources of information and entertainment. Many tab readers have education levels extending into graduate school or have professional jobs.

Tabloids characterize the typical reader as a 39-year-old, employed married woman. She might purchase more than one tab at a time—sometimes on impulse—although she is often devoted to a certain title. Tabloid studies also show that her husband reads it, too, and she is likely to pass it on to a friend.

"Pass-along" rates among tab readers are important, because they are much higher than for mainstream newspapers. As tab editors are fond of pointing out, the standard formula for newspaper readership is 2.5 people—tabloids turn out to be about twice that. After all, "you're talkin' family and all the rest of 'em," one reporter said, "and you don't go passing along the *Miami Herald* to Mr. Nelson across the way."

"We are writing for Mrs. Smith in Kansas City," *Enquirer's* Iain Calder said. "But she could be in Queens, New York, or a suburb of Chicago. Mrs. Smith is Middle America."

Tab readers are the ones who vote in the Richard Nixons and the Jimmy Carters. They are the ones who join the army and fire departments, sell shoes at the mall, and pay almost all the taxes. To ignore or trivialize this group seems a great mistake. To classify them as ignorant is arrogant.

"Everybody likes to say they don't believe what they read in tabloids. That's a basic defense mechanism," *Globe* editorial director Phil Bunton said. "But they do, and they quote tabloids to their friends, and they strew around the stories. If we screw up on a story, they're very quick to call us up and say that six months ago you said that Michael Landon was married to so and so, and this week you said he's married to someone else. So they watch and they pay attention . . . and so they believe it."

Politicians know who's reading the tabs, and George Bush is not the only one to recognize the tabloid audience.

"I don't know [if tab readers vote], but there's plenty of evidence that politicians have been very keen to give exclusive interviews to the *Enquirer* and the *Star* in the past. Reagan has. Jimmy Carter did. Ted Kennedy, especially, has made himself available to the *Enquirer* for interviews in the past. They're all aware of the power of the tabs," Bunton said.

"There's no question that the tabs are a lot more powerful, certainly, than Gannett is, and more than Knight-Ridder is. When the tabs get involved in issues they tend to get a lot more involved than 'serious' newspapers do."

Indeed, the devotion tabloids and their readers have for each other is marvelous. When the *National Examiner* reported that Polident commercial star Martha ("Bigmouth") Raye was hospitalized, she received more than 1,000 get-well cards. The *Examiner's* Tony Leggett gets more than 200 letters a day seeking his psychic assistance. Only Ann

Landers and Abigail Van Buren get more mail. Crates of letters are carted into the tabloids' offices every day and "readers' service" personnel make sure each person receives an answer to his or her question—no matter how bizarre or "stupid."

The tabloids take their readers seriously, and the readers return the favor.

As tab editor Billy Burt put it: "Well, ya think on it. There's no less than 100 million working people in this land. How many have got degrees? How many are professional? So what happens to the great unwashed who don't read the *Washington Post*, who live in fuckin' Idaho, who can't get the goddamn *New York Times* except a day later? What are they supposed to do? Because the guy's a redneck truck driver, does that mean he's valueless?"

According to Phil Bunton, focus group studies show that tabloid readers do not often read other newspapers. They don't get much news from the television, which they regard as depressing. So it's safe to assume that the 50 million folks out there, the Mr. and Mrs. Smiths of America, are relying on the supermarket tabloids not only as a main source of news and entertainment, but perhaps their sole source of news and entertainment. And these people are anything but valueless to tabloid editors.

For tabloids, the bottom line is money. None of them have any hesitation in saying this. Other journalists may wax philosophical about their sacred trust and duty to the public, but not tabloid editors.

An editor told me he once uncovered information that Bob Hope was having sex with Miss World. Reporting this, however, "would have been like setting fire to fuckin' Santa Claus. You run a story like that and you lose 100,000 copies." Tabloids tend to stay away from anything controversial. Take a stand on good versus evil? Sure, all the time. Take a stand on abortion? Show more than an occasional woman in a swimming suit? Forget it. A move like that might chop sales in half. Supermarket owners might toss the paper out of the store forever, or a million angry moms might call up an advertiser and complain.

The supermarket tabloids, unlike their far raunchier British counterparts, like to make sure their publications can be left around the house for any little kid to pick up without upsetting his parents. Although some people may be embarrassed to be seen with a tabloid, it's not something you need to carry around in a brown paper bag.

This conservatism is due to the tabs' utter dependence on their readers, who buy the paper each week without subscribing. To risk offending them (or boring them) is to risk financial disaster and, for tabloids, that's a risk they take every single week.

This is not to say that they never take chances. Editors at the *National Examiner* were gambling big stakes when they chose to start running stories about "disgraced preacher" Jim Bakker, who was sentenced to federal prison for fraud. How many *Examiner* readers would be offended by an article containing even the slightest attack on someone who was once a very popular preacher? Tentatively at first, the *Examiner* experimented then ran endless stories trashing Bakker. Eventually no story was too cruel. Many stories were fabricated, such as one claiming he had a prison boyfriend named "Peaches." Unflattering photos of Bakker with his face screwed up in tears fairly accused him of being demented.

"The only people with clout in the tabloid industry are the readers," tab editor Bob Smith said. "And let's face it, people that try and dictate tabloid policy . . . there's been a helluva lot of tabloids come on the scene and failed. It's the marketplace. You put stuff on the cover that they don't wanna read; they're not gonna buy. So you're gonna go down the toilet."

So much for the theory that a few crafty brains are masterminding the reading material of millions to gain mind control over the population.

Then there's the typical reader of the more far-out and "unbelievable" tabloids like the *Weekly World News*, which consists of either extra-sensationalized stories lifted from other newspapers or stories made up from the start. Especially since the *Sun* lost a lawsuit against an old lady in Arkansas and was forced to admit tabs do invent some stories, both the *WWN* and the *Sun* have become more outlandish.

Either their readers are some of the most gullible people on earth or there is something else going on. Judging by reader mail to the *Sun*, I can guarantee a segment of the population truly believes the fake stories planted in tabloids.

How can you sell a million copies of lies to people every single week? Author S. Elizabeth Bird calls a good segment of tab buyers "self-conscious" readers who read tabs for their "irony." In her book *For Enquiring Minds: A Cultural Study of Supermarket Tabloids*, she studied tabloid content and readers and found a number of people enjoyed the "direct, stereotyped" language in the tabloids. Such readers often read tabs as a kind of inside joke with themselves, but make "absolutely sure that no one could think they are taking them seriously."

This "self-conscious irony" seems to be the general cant of mainstream reporters who write articles about the tabloids. Tab people find such reporters more than a little hypocritical and lazy. "If we're 'that bad' then why are they trying to do it?" complained John Blackburn, formerly of the *Globe*. "Why are they so interested in what we're doing that they report what we're doing? I'm not talking about the *Columbia Journalism Review*. I'm talking about the *Washington Post*. Why is it once every two months somebody wants to come in here and do an interview on the tabloids? The same anecdotes about the tabloids, the same old tired stuff they've been doing over and over and we can't figure out what—are they looking for a job? I mean what are they here for? Wanna hear the same anecdotes? Go take it from the clips."

Indeed most "journalistic" stories about the supermarket tabs do repeat the same anecdotes. They also repeat whatever they're told without much questioning and without much checking.

♦ ♦ ♦
7

Lawsuits and Checkbook Journalism

Many people believe tabloids are constantly sued. They think Carol Burnett delivered a punishing defeat to the *National Enquirer* and cost them a bundle. They think tabloids are constantly libeling someone and that stars just hate to be in the tabs.

That's all wrong.

Tabloids are hardly ever sued. Hollywood attorney Vincent Chieffo advises his celebrity clients not to bring suit against tabloids. It's just not worth the effort. "It's the scorpion defense," he explained. "You don't attack a scorpion because you're going to get stung." Because tabs love to litigate. If you sue them, be prepared to shell out hundreds of thousands in legal fees, to have everyone in the world subpoenaed, and to have court orders obtained that will open up your personal life to even harsher scrutiny. And don't forget to have a good case.

In those rare cases when tabloids go to court, they don't lose. The *Globe* did not lose a single case until 1992—not a bad record for 38 years of pushing libel laws to their limits.

Even when stars "win" they don't win. In 1981 Carol Burnett did get a $1.6 million judgment against the *Enquirer*. Years and many appeals later, that judgment was reduced to $200,000. The *Enquirer* was limbering up for another court battle when Burnett settled for an undisclosed sum. Her legal fees alone must have cost her more than the reduced judgment. One source estimated her settlement at around $50,000. The lawsuit was a hellish ordeal for Burnett, who didn't sound too cheerful when she later said, "You have to go through the falling down in order to learn to walk. It helps to know that you can survive it. The next time something bad happens you can say, 'I will survive.'"

When Cher took the *Star* to court in 1988, suing for $30 million, she ended up getting just $400,000. Then the federal appeals court reversed the lower court's ruling and threw the whole case out against the *Star*. Cher got nothing.

Stars use the tabloids, leaking personal gossip to promote their sagging careers. Agents will often arrange for a celebrity to be interviewed by a tabloid in exchange for an agreement to cover lesser-known talent. Before suing the *Star* and becoming a tabloid-hater, Cher frequently offered herself to the *Star* when she first struck out on her own. Shirley Jones' husband, agent Marty Ingels, who later sued the tabloids and lead a Hollywood crusade to "smash" the tabloids, used to be a reliable source of inside information about the Hollywood scene.

"If it takes me a hundred years, I will right a disastrous wrong by a newspaper in which careers are mutilated every week," Ingels crowed. He convinced Steve McQueen to sue the *Enquirer* for reporting that McQueen had terminal cancer. McQueen denied the awful accusation and joined the "anti-*Enquirer* army." McQueen died of lung cancer well before the crusade was finished. Ingels' suit was reduced from his proposed $20 million in 1979 to a closed-door agreement that covered his more than $300,000 in legal fees and left him just enough to buy a sailboat in 1984. Ingels didn't seem to prosper much from the deal, but he still claimed, "We're talking satisfaction here."

Sometimes it seems celebs sue the tabloids just to cast doubt on their reporting, not caring if they lose but hoping the extra coverage will boost their careers. Dionne Warwick first sued the *Globe* for $30 million when it reported she had a jawbone disease. When she suddenly dropped the suit a *Globe* lawyer pointed out, "The retraction speaks for itself."

Shortly before their divorce, Liz Taylor and Senator John Warner threatened to sue the *Enquirer* for reporting their marriage was crumbling. The two parted, apparently, before they could get around to attacking the tab.

An L.A. judge dismissed a $12-million lawsuit against the *Globe* brought by Scott Thorson, who claimed to be the late Liberace's boy-lover. Thorson claimed the whole thing was a set-up by his half-brother. It's worth remembering that Liberace once won a libel suit in Britain against a paper that insinuated the flashy piano player was gay.

In 1990, before Marla Maples became Mrs. Trump, her mom and aunt sued the *Enquirer* over publishing a story headlined "CAUGHT! TRUMP AND HIS MISTRESS." Obviously, this case, too, has never gone forward.

When Phillip Michael Thomas (Detective Tubbs on *Miami Vice*) saw the *Enquirer* had published the fact that his brother Marcus was doing 27 years for raping and robbing three women, he sued for $10 million and got zip.

Caroll O'Connor blustered at the *National Enquirer* for publishing the many rumors that he was itching to dump his *In the Heat of the Night* costar Howard Rollins for the actor's chronic misbehavior. O'Connor was so pissed he told reporters in 1989, "You know, at first I thought I might sue the *Enquirer* for $20 million. Now I think I'm going to sue for $100 million!" Since then, Rollins was fired for, among other things, drunk driving while wearing women's clothing and using drugs. O'Connor shows no signs of having recently come into a ton of money.

In late 1990 Roseanne Barr went so far as to seek $10 million in compensatory damages and $25 million in punitive damages in federal court using the Racketeer Influenced and Corrupt Organizations (RICO) Act as her weapon. According to the suit, the *Enquirer* allegedly was involved in "a scheme to obtain the private papers and effects of celebrities by inducing and paying persons to steal such information and transport it in interstate commerce." These heavy-duty lawsuits were filed against the *National Enquirer* and the *Sun* for publishing four letters she had written to Tom Arnold—"private, written letters and outpourings of love and affection." The court case went nowhere.

Handling of Celebrity Interviews

INTER OFFICE MEMO

▮▮▮▮▮▮▮▮▮▮▮▮▮▮▮▮▮▮▮▮▮▮▮

▮▮▮▮▮▮▮▮▮▮▮▮▮▮ • BOCA RATON, FL ▮▮▮▮▮▮▮

FROM: ▮▮▮▮▮▮▮   **DATE:** May 12, 1989

TO: All Writers   **SUBJECT:** Legal Guidelines
      All Desk Persons
      ▮▮▮▮▮▮▮
      ▮▮▮▮▮▮▮

     cc: ▮▮▮▮▮▮
          ▮▮▮▮▮▮

Attached is a concise summary of important legal memos
distributed by myself, ▮▮▮▮, and/or ▮▮▮▮▮▮ over the last
six years. The material will be familiar to some, but new
to most of the writing staff.

In recent weeks we've had legal problems -- fortunately, with
no consequences -- in three particular areas: the use of
books as sources, names and identities of sources in celebrity
stories particularly, and in the writing of crime stories
which are still pending a verdict.

Basically, these problems could be remedied by careful rewriting of older books without using large unedited chunks
of quotes; by penciling in the source (and his or her credentials) in the margin next to the relevant quotes in celeb
stories; and by more use of the words "alleged," "reportedly,"
and "suspect" in crime stories.

Thanks for your cooperation in these important matters.

Enquirer editor Iain Calder noted, "Any legal action against this publication under RICO is so ridiculous that it is clear this is just another pathetic publicity stunt by Roseanne." The court threw out her RICO claim. Much of Barr's rancor seems to stem from the tabloid discovery of the child she gave up for adoption before she became rich and famous.

The tabs are so good at getting personal information on celebrities that in recent years stars have taken to "outing" themselves just so the tabs won't get the "satisfaction."

The most famous of these was when *Starsky & Hutch*'s Paul Michael Glaser and his wife, Elizabeth, hurried to the *Los Angeles Times* on 29 August 1989 with the story of their daughter's death from AIDS. They did this after the *National Enquirer* told them they had the death certificate and were preparing to run the story, then refused to keep it secret. Even in death (Elizabeth has since expired from AIDS herself) the tabloids learned to steer away from her litigious threats. Though they had it on good authority that Ms. Glaser was becoming demented and using as many as ten fentanyl patches per day to quell her intense pain, the *Enquirer* politely waited until she was dead to write about it.

The Glasers are not the only ones whose highly aggressive postures have managed to mute tabloid coverage. Tom Selleck, too, has earned a reputation for leaping into battle with any tabloid that so much as mentions his name. When the *Globe* ran a *flattering* story about the actor in 1989, Selleck went to war. Only behind-the-scenes lawyering and the digging up of a little family dirt managed to halt his attack. This strategy cost a lot of money, but at least Selleck has bought the silence of the tabloids. For now.

Kate Jackson (always a big tabloid seller during her days as one of *Charlie's Angels*) went public with the news of her breast cancer and impending mastectomy not only to reach out to other women in the same situation but also "to save inquiring minds 50 cents." Comedian and talk-show hostess Jenny Jones did much the same thing in early 1992 after she realized it was a matter of time before her botched breast surgeries would lead to a double mastectomy—and quite possibly a tabloid story. To get some control over the news, Jones went to *People* with an exclusive. She didn't seem to mind that on March 2 her story appeared right beside the tabloids in the same checkout lines.

After the *Star* ran a story on 22 August 1989 that described Demi Moore's sordid past, her "slide into alcohol abuse," and "her violent scrapes with the law," her mom, Virginia Moore, decided to write a tell-all book that would leave the tabloids nothing more to write about. She may have been doing it for the money, since other tabloid reports (that didn't result in lawsuits) say Demi's mom is impoverished and her daughter refuses to share her wealth.

In the Courtroom

At times, tabloids have been in the front lines, fighting journalistic battles that have benefited all media. After the *Globe* revealed the name of the alleged rape victim at the Kennedy compound in 1991, it had to defend itself in Florida court. The law was deemed unconstitutional and thrown out of court, establishing a precedent that effectively unmuzzled the press in Florida and possibly elsewhere.

The *Globe* is fighting an appeal in a California court that, if it wins, will broaden a journalistic legal tenet known as "neutral reportage." This concept was established in 1977 in a suit against the National Audubon Society and the *New York Times*. The *Times* was sued after a National Audubon Society official called three scientists "paid liars" and the *Times* reported his comments. The court found that the paper's right to report the remarks was protected under the First Amendment. Neutral reportage protects newspapers from libel suits if they are merely reporting the assertions of a person whom they believe was in a position to know.

In the *Globe* case, brought to court in the spring of 1993, a Pakistani named Khalid Khawar was accused of having been involved in the murder of Robert Kennedy. In 1988 the accusation was made by former CIA agent Robert Morrow in his book *The Senator Must Die*. The *Globe* reviewed the book and repeated the accusation—making very sure not to endorse the claim.

The judge was miffed at the original hearing, called the complaint "a turkey," and nearly threw it out. But the plaintiff's attorney insisted that the testimony of a *Globe* reporter was crucial to his case—testimony that had yet to be heard. The judge decided to let it go to trial, "because I want to see what you're able to establish through him that does you any good, because you're drowning here," he lectured

Khawar's attorney. "Maybe you can blow up your Mae West and last awhile longer. Do you follow me?"

As it turns out, the *Globe* reporter's testimony was of no importance to the plaintiff's case. The jury, too, seemed unimpressed.

Although a civil case requires only nine of twelve jurors to agree with the plaintiff, the jury took four days of deliberations (in which screaming was heard coming from their room) to find against the tabloid, awarding Khawar $1.17 million. The *Globe* immediately appealed. In September 1996 the case was accepted for review by the California Supreme Court. It is likely the case will be overturned on appeal—no problem for the tabs, who have been down this road before.

The doctrine of neutral reportage was further strengthened and clarified in the Second District Court of Appeals. The mainstream press may not like it, but the tabloids go to bat for everyone. Like Larry Flynt's landmark case reestablishing the right of the press to satirize public figures, the hero may not fit the image the establishment may prefer—but all the media benefits.

Lawyers and Libel

The *Enquirer* has in-house lawyers while the *Globe* retains the services of Chicago-based Deutsch, Levy & Engel. Each week the firm flies a lawyer to Palm Beach and puts an attorney in a plush hotel room for a few days while he or she goes over the *Globe*, the *Examiner* and the *Sun* with a magnifying glass. Libel is painstakingly avoided. Just to make sure, all pages are subsequently faxed to the Chicago office for another look. Each page of the *Globe* is read three times by at least two lawyers before it is approved.

This combination of feistiness and caution means the tabloids are hardly ever involved in lawsuits, which is not to say they never have legal troubles. When they screw up, they screw up big. In June 1984 the *Globe* erroneously reported that Yusef Islam (formerly Cat Stevens) was aiding the Ayatollah Khomeini and wore a hair shirt while begging in the streets of Teheran. Since Yusef Islam had never even been to Iran, he sued the tab and the *Globe* quickly settled out of court.

Another reason the tabloids are seldom in court because they typically pay off. Even if they think they'll win a case, they'll often figure out how much the suit would cost them to defend and then offer that amount to settle. This was Globe Communication's policy as articulated by Mike Kahane, the company's chief lawyer, in an April 1990 meeting with staffers of the *National Examiner*.

The Tabs' Biggest Blunder

To date, the worst screw-up came from the normally ultracautious *Sun*, whose editor, John Vader, was almost obsessive about not defaming a living person or otherwise risking legal trouble. In the 2 October 1990 issue, the *Sun* ran a story featuring a woman who, the paper claimed, was 101 years old and pregnant. Vader had found a photo in the files of a spunky 86-year-old newscarrier in Arkansas (she was shown riding a bicycle in the picture) named Nellie Mitchell, who was featured in a 1980 *National Examiner* story. He made the wrong assumption that woman must be dead. Nobody bothered to double-check this, another uncommon blunder. Perhaps her age, coupled with her residence in small-town Arkansas, made him feel confident enough to make up the story's premise, assigning it to writer Manny Silver.

Silver concocted a story to go with the picture, datelined it in an Australian town and put the file into the bin. Nellie Mitchell turned out not only to be alive, but was almost immediately informed of her presence on the *Sun*'s cover. She filed suit and apparently did not accept whatever offer the parent company, Globe Communications, made to her, so the case went to trial.

That trial changed tabloids in a major way, because, for the first time, tab editors, writers and lawyers openly and explicitly admitted they ran completely faked stories. Until then this was something everyone "knew" but could not prove. Mainstream articles about the tabloids before this trial were very careful never to directly accuse the tabloids of making up stories out of whole cloth (were they afraid of lawsuits?). And at the tabs it was one of the only codes of conduct reporters obeyed. When the tabloid used the "all in fun" fake story defense, it was no longer a secret.

Nellie Mitchell's lawyers brought in Paul Greenberg, a Pulitzer-Prize-winning editorial writer, and Bob McCord, a former senior editor of the *Arkansas Gazette*, to testify that faked new stories were a violation of "journalistic ethics." Globe Communications countered with its local experts. Bob Douglas, a former managing editor of the *Gazette*, and the chairman of the University of Arkansas journalism department both testified the *Sun* hadn't violated any "journalistic ethics" at all—since the *Sun* wasn't even journalism.

For once mainstream snootiness came in handy.

But the defense failed and Mitchell won a judgment of more than $1 million, courtesy of a jury of her peers. This type of thing just doesn't play well in Mountain Home, Arkansas, and there was no way to get the venue changed. Although Nellie Mitchell would have probably settled for whatever sum the tabloid was offering (more than $50,000), it seems her friends and relatives urged her on to go to trial—the last thing Globe Corp. wanted to do.

Blurring Fact and Fiction

The trial confirmed an interesting feature about such stories. The line between fiction and reality is so thin and arbitrary, even the writers of the fake stories (called "wing-its" at the *Sun*) could not always distinguish between stories they had invented and ones that were real and simply culled from obscure newspapers. Silver testified he could no longer remember whether another story in the same issue ("Hit Man Kills Agent for $500") was true or made-up. However, an implausible story by another writer, "Farmer Becomes Millionaire Making Whips for Wife-Beaters," turned out to be true. The line between fact and fiction at the tabloids is so blurred that it requires a battery of lawyers to protect tab editors from themselves!

At one editorial meeting I attended in 1991, attorney Mike Kahane patiently explained to editor Joe West why he could not publish a story about Michael Jackson and Jack Nicholson planning a trip to the moon if there was no truth to it. West's idea to attribute the story to "sources close to the stars" cut no ice with the lawyer. When writing about a living person, he explained, it was imperative that the story be true or that at least reasonable steps to verify it had been taken.

Perhaps after editing the *Weekly World News* for so long, West had lost his grip of the real and unreal. After each explanation by the lawyer, West kept insisting the lawyer's job was not to tell him what stories to write, but to keep him out of trouble. Of course he could write a story about Michael Jackson's trip to the moon. Finally Kahane told him, "If you try to run a story like that, I will kill it. It will not run." End of discussion.

West was noticeably irritated by the lawyer's refusal to help make up a story. This kind of confrontation between editor and lawyer has led to many heated arguments and power plays.

One of Globe Corp.'s attorneys was fired after she became disliked by a couple of editors. They felt she kept "nagging" about libelous statements and falsehoods getting into the paper. Editors were indignant. Every time an error was caught or a story with no source was found, it was thrown back. Editors Paul Levy of the *Globe* and Lee Harrison of the *Examiner* resorted to making up fictitious sources to "solve" this problem. There were times when Harrison simply ordered someone to fake a source to get the lawyers to shut up, according to then-*Examiner* copy editor Morag Dick. At the tabloids it is not uncommon to fake quotes and stories, but it's almost impossible to catch them at it.

Where other publications may get away with lifting several pages of a book to review it, tabloids are very strict about using another person's words. At the same meeting where Joe West locked horns with Kahane, a memo was distributed and carefully explained to every staffer. Book reviews could contain no more than one or two paragraphs from the original source. In addition, books were to be reviewed in a positive light. This was so stressed at Globe Corp. that many editors believe such restrictions are the law, not just the advice of their vigilant attorney.

It may seem ridiculous to instruct a reporter not to copy a story verbatim from another publication or to "not use sly or cute innuendo to suggest some misbehavior that you do not intend to describe explicitly," but it is by not ignoring the obvious that tabloids avoid a lot of legal troubles.

The Tabloid with No Brakes

The only noteworthy feature of Paul Azzaria and the *News Extra* are the lawsuits brought against it. One lawsuit in particular examines how a tabloid can cross the line from sensationalistic extrapolation into outright libel.

The *News Extra* was another Montreal creation connected with the Globe Communications. Until it committed suicide a few years after its inception, it did a credible job as the newest member on the checkout stand racks. By 1987 the supermarket tabloid market had long been saturated and was in the hands of the six tabs we still have today. The days of ephemeral competitors with names like *Confidential Flash* or the *National Exploiter* were over. Rack space came at a premium, and it seems astonishing that this upstart paper could claim a fairly respectable circulation of 200,000 distributed through 32,000 outlets across the U.S. and Canada.

The paper's publisher was Joe Azaria's younger brother Paul, who had added an extra z to his last name. Paul had worked at least briefly with his brother at *Midnight* and presumably had the right connections to get another tab going.

There was something wrong with *News Extra* from the very beginning. Its tiny staff didn't do much original reporting and seemed to rely mainly on rewrites of stories published in other tabloids. They also didn't pay too well. A front-page story might get the writer a whole fifty bucks! There was nothing in the paper to make it compete with the other six tabloids. By rights it shouldn't have been there in the first place.

Then came the blockbuster stories—in the summer of 1991 it ran a story accusing Rod Stewart of playing around on his new wife. The story resulted in a lawsuit brought by Stewart. In September it ran an exclusive story revealing macho actor Sylvester Stallone had abused steroids so much he'd become permanently impotent. The paper said Sly had recently gotten a penile implant to correct the problem. Stallone objected, saying the story wasn't true, and he filed his own lawsuit.

The new tab was defending itself in court against the two suits and all seemed business as usual for a tabloid. Then, in March of '92, the little tab had another blockbuster story—this time about Oprah Winfrey. According to the paper, Oprah's boyfriend, Stedman Graham, had had gay sex with his cousin, Carlton Jones. Jones—a former "male model" and at the time working in the fast-food industry at an entry-level position—was quoted throughout the story. He said Stedman had "left me broken-hearted" by going back to Oprah. The article speculated that the revelation of Stedman's alleged homosexuality might disrupt any wedding plans Oprah had with him.

Naturally, Oprah and Stedman filed suit—for $300 million. They said none of the story was true. This is par for the tabloid course, and the paper began considering ways to defend against the charge. Its tactics turned out to be quite novel; the *News Extra* didn't appear to take the normal steps any other tabloid would take to defend itself.

Normally, a tab would start filing motions to drag the suit out as long as possible. Lawyers would file for discovery in the hope that they could find even worse things about Oprah or Stedman that could be used to legally blackmail them into dropping the suit. They would file motions to dismiss or to change venue. Even if they wouldn't do any of this, there is no rational explanation for why they didn't at least get their chief source, Carlton Jones, on the phone and prep him to testify.

Except it looks as if the paper had never spoken to Carlton or anyone else about the story. As events unfolded it became apparent that the story was stolen from the files of the *Globe*. A reporter at that paper had spoken to the burger-slinger and had determined—despite his juicy allegations—that there wasn't enough to run the story. The *Globe* had killed it. It looks as if someone had then fed the story to *News Extra*, which made some slight changes in the quotes and ran the story.

This presented some serious problems for the paper's defense in court. There didn't seem to be any good way to squirm out of the charge. They were facing settlement time and financial ruin.

The paper simply folded and fled town. Oprah went ahead with her suit and won handily in a default judgment when no one from the *News Extra* showed up in court. However, there doesn't appear to be anyone to shake down for the $300 million. As for Azzaria, he professes to be amazed by the lawsuit in the first place. "They're just unreal, these folks," he told the *Montreal Gazette*. "When you hurt their feelings, you know." That was the last Azzaria had to say on the matter and no one else is talking either. In the tabloid world, the *News Extra* is not spoken of anymore. It is as if it had vanished from the minds of people in Tabloid Valley as completely as it did in Montreal.

◆ ◆ ◆
8

Gangsters, Spies and the National Enquirer

It's easy to find overt connections between the tabloids and the CIA, the Mafia and other highly motivated and political organizations. The *Enquirer*'s founder and longtime publisher, Generoso Pope, worked as a CIA officer and was intimately connected with Mafia figures like Frank Costello, who in turn was closely tied to anti-Castro Cubans, the CIA and Israeli intelligence services. The CIA, Sophia Loren and the Mafia were the three topics said to be forbidden at the *National Enquirer* during Pope's reign.

Pope "invented" the supermarket tab by becoming the first tabloid publisher to sell in grocery store checkout lines. The *National Enquirer* set the tone for all the tabs that followed. Even the phrase "like something out of the *National Enquirer*" has come to mean something far-fetched, unbelievable or sensational.

Mainstream reporters "covering" the tabloids loved to interview Pope because he knew what they had come for and he gave it to them in spades. He was the archetypal self-made man, son of an Italian immigrant who came to America with just $4 in his pocket. By his wits, shrewd analysis of his readership and dumb luck, Pope was able to transform an ailing and doomed New York rag into a nationwide magazine with a circulation that topped 6.5 million in the early 1970s (also in 1977, when Elvis died). His penchant for getting the story at any cost is legendary. He thought nothing of sending a team of 20 or 30 reporters to cover a Hollywood scandal. He never winced at shelling out tens of thousands of dollars for a story, then killing it at the last second because he just didn't feel it was right for the *Enquirer*.

He offered bonuses to his already highly paid staffers if they came up with the week's most far-out idea. He lavished his reporters with princely expense accounts, paid exorbitant sums for information and still never fell prey to the evils of filthy lucre. Gene Pope lived for the *Enquirer*. Far more interested in expanding the paper's readership than its profits, he pulled out all the stops to seek out and keep customers. Although his $12 million annual TV ad campaign increased circulation, it was not cost-effective. (It was axed upon his death in 1988.) "It was like stapling three dollars to the last 150,000 copies," Michael Boylan complained, once he had taken over. Pope didn't care.

"I can eat only so many hamburgers," Pope would say when questioned why he didn't seek to expand his empire or pamper himself. He drove beat-up cars to work, chain-smoked Kents and worked six days a week. Pope's gardener told visiting reporters his boss would sometimes come out in his pajamas with a ruler to make sure the grass around the *Enquirer* was exactly four inches high. Pope ran a tight ship.

Lantana, Florida, the town that hosted his paper, benefited from his extravagant generosity. He funded local charities and hospitals and blew more than a million dollars each Christmas to have "the world's tallest Christmas tree" brought from a special railroad car from Washington State.

This is just one side of Generoso Pope Jr.—the official side—as manicured as his lawn. He could be a hard boss. He approved or rejected every story idea that went into his paper, and he scanned each issue for typos or layout errors. A slacker could not get by for long. Pope's habit of firing anyone who failed in his assigned task was as well-known as his habit of rehiring them once they had been exiled for a few months in Palm Beach County. This encompassed the "dark side" of Pope, the ugly truth reporters were allowed to ferret out. It was not the official *Enquirer* line—not officially.

Outside reporters writing about the *Enquirer* found it relatively easy to discover the enormous newsroom pressure to "get the story." They saw the evidence of mass and capricious firings, of deliberate humiliation between rivals. Pope used to pit "teams" of reporters against each other for the same story, with the winners getting to keep their jobs. The current editor-in-chief, Iain Calder, is so cold-hearted that employees call him "Ice Pick" to his face. Calder brags that "at least it shows [I] won't stab you in the back." The intense competition has led to heavy alcohol abuse and suicide among some tabloid reporters.

All this "dirt" was spoon-fed to mainstream reporters.

By giving outsiders juicy, even mean things to say about him, Pope placated them and they left him alone. *60 Minutes* showed up to "expose" the *Enquirer* and its quirky owner more than once, only to be fed a little bit of damning information and sent packing. Never once did anyone look into Pope's background or question whether what he told them was the truth. Mainstream reporters proved themselves as gullible as anyone else. Starstruck by Pope and the glittering image of the *Enquirer*, no one thought to verify his words or find out if there was, perhaps, another story besides the one they were telling.

Behind the Cover

Another story about Pope parallels the one normally told about him. This chapter will enumerate interesting facts about the man and his newspaper and let the reader draw his or her conclusions. Just as I challenge the assumption that supermarket tabloids like the *National Enquirer* are of little or no consequence in American society, I also challenge the idea that Generoso Pope—and indeed anyone who owns or seeks to own a supermarket tabloid—is or was an inconsequential buffoon.

Generoso Pope's father was an Italian immigrant, but whether or not he really came to the United States broke is hearsay. Pope Sr. was the founder of the Italian-language newspaper *Il Progresso*, which influenced large numbers of Italian Americans in America—especially in and around New York City and along the East Coast. The paper was of sufficient interest to the U.S. government that the Office of Strategic Services (OSS, the predecessor of the CIA) kept it under close watch during World War II, infiltrating meetings attended by Pope Sr. and keeping a sharp eye on its editorial policies. Pope Sr. was rumored to be a fascist sympathizer, but reports to the government showed he was a staunch supporter of Italy's king and welcomed good relations with the United States, especially once the fascists had been routed.

During Generoso Pope Jr.'s life, his connections to the Mob were well-known. They were mentioned—then skirted—by nearly everyone. Perhaps reporters feared the consequences of revealing the extent to which Pope was connected to the Mob. Maybe it seemed enough just to mention the association; after all, it added to the man's mystique. Maybe reporters thought too highly of the Mafia or of the U.S. government's espionage agencies to connect them with someone as laughable as the publisher of a sleazy supermarket tabloid.

If so, then Pope had played them like fiddles. Again.

Generoso Pope was anything but inconsequential. Pope attended high school at New York's Horace Mann School for Boys with future right-wing lawyer Roy Cohn, who often had young Gene over for dinner at his mother's house. He then went to MIT and graduated in 1947 with an engineering degree at the age of 19. He was something of a prodigy, if not an outright genius.

According to his résumé, Pope accomplished all this while editing *Il Progresso*. He also served as vice president of the family's sand and gravel business, characterized as a "racket" by the FBI (which kept files on the Pope family until at least the '60s). As cited in Pope's self-written biography in *Who's Who*, the young engineer went to work for the CIA in 1951.

"I did something called psychological warfare," Pope told reporters, "but I can't tell you anything more." And he didn't. And neither did they. After all, he worked for the CIA for just that one year. Nobody probed what he did at the CIA, and nobody questioned whether someone could drop in on the intelligence community, do a little psychological warfare, "become disenchanted with the bureaucracy," and then drop out, severing all ties with the agency.

Considering that Pope's next step was to purchase a newspaper in 1952, it seems highly unlikely that the 25-year-old spy was merely job-hopping. He supposedly financed the purchase of the Hearst-owned *New York Enquirer* for $75,000, putting up $20,000 as a down payment. The 20 grand was said to have come variously from a bank, a banker, a friend, or mobster Frank Costello. In Pope's words the loan was at "zero interest." He claimed he was unaware that the paper was a week away from bankruptcy at the time he bought it. So much for the shrewd investor.

Despite the bad financial health of his paper, he borrowed $250,000 in personal loans over the next five years. By 1957 things began to stabilize; by 1958 the paper was beginning to show a profit. His business sense seems to have had less to do with shrewdness than with good connections, especially for money. A penniless person simply cannot borrow a quarter of a million dollars over five years without any collateral—unless he wasn't borrowing at all.

Generoso Pope's links with government agencies and known mobsters is undisputed. In 1950 the *New York Times* reported that Pope lost his title as honorary police deputy in the city, which entitled him to special parking privileges and snappy salutes from police officers. Apparently, Acting Mayor Impellitteri was punishing Pope for his role as an "emissary of Frank Costello, gambler and racketeer" and for publicly saying he was backing New York Supreme Court Justice Ferdinand Pecora for mayor—just as Frank Costello was. Impellitteri was explicit that it was Pope's pro-Costello, pro-Pecora remarks that got him booted off the ceremonial police force.

Pope's enduring relationship with Costello, and by extension, the gangster's associates, helps clarify aspects of Pope's career that would otherwise be chalked up to blind luck or uncanny business acumen. That Pope was close to Costello is clear: Costello was godfather to Pope's children. On 2 May 1957, the night a hit man botched his assassination of Costello, Pope had just finished dinner with Frank and a mysterious character named Phillip Kennedy. The bullet failed to penetrate the mobster's head, and neither Costello, Kennedy, nor Pope said they saw a thing.

Investigation into the Existence of the Mafia

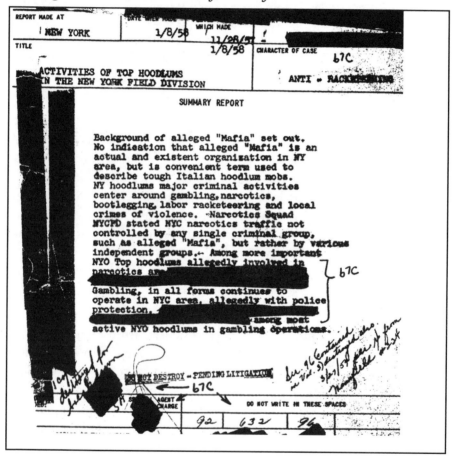

Other Mafia figures Pope admitted acquaintance with were Joseph Profaci and Albert Anastasia. Anastasia was gunned down in his barber's chair shortly after Costello's head got creased during an assassination attempt.

Results of Investigation into Pope's Mafia Involvement

Office Memorandum • UNITED STATES GOVERNMENT

TO : SAC, NEW YORK (94- DATE: 5/24/60

FROM : SUPERVISOR ████████████ b7c

SUBJECT: GENEROSO POPE

    Supervisor ████████ of WFO called me today and
advised that the top hoodlum from Chicago,██████████████   b7c
had stayed in a Washington, D. C., hotel last night in a
room registered to G. POPE, 1151 Broadway, New York.
██████████ was of the opinion that this may be the son of
GENEROSO POPE. He was interested in obtaining the first name
of the son as well as the dob so that he could check passport
records, obtain a photograph, and possibly make an identification.

    A review of the files in NYO did not reflect this
information. I contacted██████████████████ who subsequently
returned my call and informed me that GENEROSO POPE had three sons
FORTUNE ROBERT POPE; ANTHONY JOHN POPE and GENEROSO PAUL POPE, JR.,   b7c
dcd - 1/13/27; address - 135 East 74th St., Manhattan, telephone
BU 8-3644.

    I called Supervisor ████████ and furnished him with
this information, at which time he informed me that the possibility
exists that the person ████████ was with in the Washington, D.C.   b7c
hotel may have been a local hood; however, a case had been
opened and a lead would be forthcoming to NYO to conduct
investigation in the vicinity of 1151 Broadway.

In 1976, in a lame attempt to investigate *Enquirer*–Mafia connections, CBS's Mike Wallace asked Pope during a *60 Minutes* episode if Mafia money had bankrolled the *Enquirer*. Pope told Wallace, "I think it's pretty obvious to anyone that understands or reads or knows anything about this organization [the Mafia], whatever it is, that if there were [Mafia money behind the *Enquirer*] there still would be. Because they never let go once they get their hooks into you, and that obviously has not happened."

Tough investigative journalist Wallace seemed satisfied with the "obviousness" Pope claimed. Pope's insight into how lasting a Mafia connection is was not considered any further.

Pope and the CIA

In 1950, a year before Gene Pope entered the CIA, the spy agency started the Massachusetts Institute of Technology Center of International Studies (MIT-CIS). In 1952 this center was headed by Max Millikan, director of the CIA's Office of National Estimates. In 1955 the CIA began "Project Brushfire," in which Millikan and others studied "the political, psychological, economic and sociological factors leading to 'peripheral wars.'"

The CIA routinely set up operatives in businesses around the world to provide "deep cover." Such agents can remain dormant for more than ten years. At times, businesses financed by the CIA have proven so profitable that the deep cover agent decides to quit working for the CIA even before he has started—paying back the capital as if it were a loan.

There's no direct evidence that Pope was involved in such a thing, but it is possible and should be considered. Leaving the CIA is not like quitting a job at the local car wash.

Pope must have had his enemies, too, as recently uncovered documents show both he and his father were under investigation for years by the FBI, apparently because of his extensive Mafia connections. For some reason, the Immigration and Naturalization Service took an interest in his foreign employees in the early '80s.

The CIA has files on Generoso Pope, too, but most of them (like those still held by the FBI) are either impossible to obtain or heavily censored.

Psychological Warfare

Pope freely admitted he worked in psychological warfare, or "psy-ops." Psychological warfare uses propaganda techniques to influence people's thoughts and opinions. Media is both the target and the medium of most propaganda, and newspapers and broadcasting are the most essential forums.

Most hard-sell sales techniques make use of "psy-ops" to get a balking customer to make a purchase. The same techniques can be used to "turn" a secret agent, extract information, or convince someone of a certain political idea. Related techniques can be used to disseminate a general opinion among a population that serves the interests of the establishment. Red-baiting and spreading the fear of Communism, for instance, were an important part of domestic propaganda in the United States in the '50s and '60s. Before the first bomb was dropped on Baghdad in January 1991, sophisticated and not-so-sophisticated techniques had already prepared the American public to accept and endorse the bombing.

Whether one is selling vacuum cleaners or political indoctrination, an understanding of "psychological warfare" is necessary for success. And the CIA has done nearly as much as Madison Avenue in exploring ways of manipulating people's emotions.

In the '50s and '60s, when Pope's *Enquirer* was experiencing its most remarkable growth, the CIA did its most vigorous research into "mind control," some of which included bizarre and quite cruel "experiments" on unwitting people. The ability to control the thoughts of individuals and the masses was very much on the CIA agenda. Its research led to the suggestion, if not construction, of all kinds of James Bond-type gear, from electronic implants to LSD delivered by spray cans and in the payloads of mortar shells. Methods for "brainwashing," especially for planting subconscious suggestions, became almost a fetish for the CIA. Agents learned much from their experiments. One of the arts developed during this time was the practice of planting subtle disinformation among a population to try to steer public opinion.

Questionable Assignments

Pope was not the only tab reporter/editor to have worked for "the company." Other tab employees claim to have worked for either British or American intelligence agencies, including one of Pope's first employees, Bill Bates. Some observers believe the tabloids provide cover jobs for spies around the world. As one might expect in any propaganda or espionage enterprise, there are few glaring ties to such organizations. Still, such obvious signs are there and are backed up by a host of more subtle clues.

Like *Reader's Digest*, the *Enquirer* has never seemed averse to spending large amounts of money, and sending reporters into exotic areas for stories that never make it into print.

In the late '70s reporter Bob Tenney was sent to Katmandu, then up more than 18,000 feet with Sherpa guides supposedly to look for the "abominable snowman." The paper was candid about admitting Tenney's failed mission. The *Enquirer* used that anecdote to support the claim that the paper would not make up stories, twist or distort facts, or even pay someone for a particularly juicy quote.

To come back from Nepal after exploring the Himalayas without an abominable snowman story seems ludicrous. There must have been at least one person willing to say they'd seen such a thing, probably for a pittance. If not that, then surely it would have been possible to distort or even, perish the thought, *invent* some information. This seems especially true if Pope really was "a tyrannical bastard," as one of his editors once called him, who fired anyone who failed to get a story.

There are other things going on in the mountain peaks where the borders of Pakistan, India and China meet—listening devices and other spy operations, primarily. Skirmishes between the Pakistani and Indian and Chinese armies break out occasionally. Might be nice to have someone on the scene from time to time asking questions about unusual sightings, taking pictures of the area, learning the roads and paths, and so on.

Former *Enquirer* reporter John Harris once spent three months in the mid-'70s traveling the world to "find Utopia." After spending tens of thousands of dollars visiting places like Uganda (toward the end of Idi Amin's Mossad-supported reign), Harris returned home supposedly empty-handed. It's not that Harris didn't see anything, and it's not that he didn't write it all down; he did. But the *Enquirer* never ran a story on it—not even a story about how hard it was to find Utopia. It is also possible this same assignment, with the same no-story results, was repeated at least one other time.

Another *Enquirer* reporter, Tony Brenna, visited Idi Amin in the 1970s and witnessed the executions of 17 people who had their heads caved in with a sledgehammer. Later, *Enquirer* editors suggested they return to interview Amin with a psychiatrist posing as a fellow reporter to assess Amin's mental condition.

It is difficult to imagine why anyone would need to secretly analyze Idi Amin's mental health. Not only would such an analysis be difficult to perform by a non-Ugandan, one wonders what the outcome could possibly be during those days of mayhem. Would reporters write "Amin steady as a rock" or "mass executions normal behavior"?

The only information gained by an in-person interview with Amin would be detailed and subtle—probably not at all what tab readers were dying to know. A person could determine the layout of Amin's home, the length of an airstrip, the types of food he ate and what time he slept, the direction the doors opened, the number of bodyguards, and their locations. All this information is crucial to intelligence agents on covert operations and can be gained only by on-site observation.

There are other obvious connections between the CIA and Pope. One of the first reporters hired by the *Enquirer* was Bill Bates, who was also a former employee of the OSS. He spent part of World War II behind enemy lines flying low-altitude bombing missions in Burma. Bates subsequently worked for Rupert Murdoch's *Star*. Like all tabloid reporters, editors and photographers, he has moved freely between the tabs.

Tabs also employ "hardened" reporters who, having covered serious news in places like Vietnam and Biafra, are presumably acquainted with the cynical ways in which human tragedy and "news" are used. Such reporters cannot credibly fall back on the "wacky tab reporter" stereotype to shield them from closer scrutiny. Their staunch, even extreme, politics should not be overlooked. Besides the *National Review*'s underground gossip Phil Brennan, there is also Tom Valentine. Valentine used to be a tabloid reporter for the *National*

Tattler and now runs a right-wing radio show and writes a column for the *Spotlight*—a newspaper known to be variously populist and fascist.

Just as the CIA likes to recruit from Ivy League schools, the *Enquirer*, too, had a program to train Yale and Harvard graduates to become tab reporters. Ostensibly, "Project Whiz Kid" was to show that "ordinary students" could become trained reporters. I'm not sure the premise was ever in dispute. What is in dispute, however, is whether Ivy League students could be considered "ordinary."

Pope's Death

In a letter to the editor of the *Palm Beach Post* shortly after Generoso Pope's death in October 1988, local resident Eileen M. Hayes had but one complaint. In the thousands of words the paper published describing Pope's massive funeral, lavishly praising his contributions to the country, and lionizing him as a visionary, the *Post* "failed to find any mention of his most wonderful gift to the community."

The gift? The *National Enquirer* Christmas tree and the many fascinating displays that enchanted the thousands of children and adults when they filed by—skating bears, Santa's workshop, intricate trains and cable cars amid colored lights shimmering in the trees.

Alas for Hayes, that Christmas in 1988 was the last to see that famous Christmas tree. The tree was one of the first things to go when the new owners took over. "Mr. Pope was Santa Claus," admitted American Media's Boylan, "and we just can't afford to be."

In June 1989, G.P. Group, a pairing of Macfadden Holdings (named after its former owner, Bernarr Macfadden) and Boston Ventures Limited Partnership III, purchased the *Enquirer* for $412.5 million. Pope's personal fortune was $150 million at the time of his death.

Another money-saving cut instituted by American Media was the mass firing of 57 employees in a single afternoon and the obliteration of the *Enquirer's* trademark TV ad campaign ("Enquiring Minds"). Pope's death was the end of an era for the whole community. An interpreter was sent to fire the Spanish-speaking gardener who had kept the grass exactly four inches high at all times for Master Pope.

When Pope died, media baron Robert Maxwell was one of a number of international competitors who wished to purchase the valuable tabloid. Bidders also included Hachette SA, at the time the world's largest producer of magazines and reference books.

The German company Bertelsmann AG was after the *Enquirer*, too. Like Hachette, Bertelsmann is one of the five biggest media conglomerates in the world. Owned by the practically invisible Reinhard Mohn, this company has saturated Germany's media after reaching the limits of that country's law. At the time of the bidding war, Bertelsmann owned Doubleday, Bantam Books, Dell and the Literary Guild book club along with RCA and Arista records and 40 magazines.

Six years after Macfadden Holdings (now called American Media) took over the *Enquirer*, it went public, disclosing an empire of hundreds of millions of dollars, more than a dozen publications and worldwide operations. In March 1990, American Media swallowed up its rival, the *Star*, for a little more than $400 million. Since then American Media's stock is only rising in price.

◆ ◆ ◆
9

Globe Communications
Enigmas from the Frozen North

The other player in the tabloid game is Globe Communications, a private company controlled by publisher Mike Rosenbloom of Montreal. Unlike the *Enquirer*'s Generoso Pope, Rosenbloom was not a newspaper man. He's an accountant who bought the company from its founder, Joe Azaria, in 1969. Rosenbloom was a hardworking man who put himself through school by driving cabs. When he became a certified accountant, he took whatever customers he could find. Joe Azaria's fledgling pulp empire was just one of his customers.

When he was ten, Joe Azaria emigrated from Iraq to Canada before the World War II. His father was in an import-export business and the family was fairly well off. In 1954, sick of his job as a waiter and after failing to get a cub reporter position at the *Montreal Gazette*, Azaria decided to start a publication called *Midnight* with a modest capital of $16. Coaxing credit from a printer and more money from friends, Azaria and partner John Vader (who was busy writing pulp fiction for detective magazines and dreaming of a career as a playwright) used a single typewriter to produce the first issue—16 pages of fairly raunchy sex stories, nightclub gossip and pictures every bit as gory as any Mexican tabloid.

John Vader, who's now retired, remembered their humble beginnings: "The printer now owns Quebecor, the second-biggest printing empire in America. He originally started with a little printing shop with a second-hand press and Joe got him to give us credit for a couple of issues.

"Originally the paper came out only every two weeks because there were so few people. It was typed up at the office and taken down to the printer where it was typeset—manually with lead type—and set into pages. At that time we had a press run of 20,000 copies, since that was the lowest you could possibly print, for which he charged us 400 bucks for the whole thing. The idea was to get those papers on the street and collect the 400 dollars before we put the next issue to bed—and that's the way it ran for quite awhile."

Not that it wasn't a blast.

"We covered sex, show business and human interest," Vader continued. "Oh yeah, we had a lot of fun in those days. Nobody was married and nobody had anything else to do but work, and work was a party."

Asked whether it was true (as Azaria had once said) that the young sleaze peddlers would 'chase chorus girls till 5:00 in the morning,' Vader hedged. "That's reasonably true. But sometimes we did it till 5:30.

"We often used to end up at the office, and when we were there we worked. It didn't really matter what time it was. If there was a party or somebody felt like going out for a drink or somebody had a new broad to screw, I mean we just went there and when we got back we went to bed. When we woke up . . . well, some of the best ideas come that way."

The little sleaze mag, which featured plenty of prurient attractions of violence and sexual innuendo, struggled for five years. It then found success after crossing into the United States. *Midnight* followed the *Enquirer* into the supermarket checkout lines, making the appropriate changes to fit. The paper was renamed *Midnight Globe*, and as the word *midnight* became smaller and smaller on the cover, simply *Globe*.

Azaria is said to have purchased four U.S. publications to add to his little empire. Around the time the *Globe* was sold to Rosenbloom, the paper had a circulation of somewhere between half and three quarters of a million, most of which was in the United States. Azaria got $4 million from Rosenbloom and then founded the *Sunday Express*, Canada's first Sunday paper.

Six years later, apparently sick of the publishing game, Azaria sold the paper to his erstwhile creditor and printer, Pierre Peladeau.

Azaria also owned the venerable *Police Gazette*, which by that time was more than 100 years old—the granddaddy of tabloids. By 1977, the paper had nearly given up the ghost again and Azaria let it die a peaceful death.

Azaria headed for Florida, taking at least $8 million with him. He later settled in Costa Rica and became boss of a 607-hectare chunk of rain forest. He partially transformed it into a pepper plantation, sharing an idyllic life with his wife in a "rambling" thatch-roofed house that lacked electricity for the first four years.

Azaria plans to write a book about his days in Montreal, hanging out with the city's noted mobsters. Like Pope's saga, Azaria's life is more than meets the eye—it's difficult to know exactly where the official story and the real story mesh. His mobster connections are probably at least as interesting as Pope's—but more nebulous. It seems at least one of his publishing arms, called Beta Publications, specialized in pornography—an enterprise which may or may not be continuing today under Rosenbloom. But not too many people talk about Azaria.

Vader reluctantly admitted that Azaria was acquainted with Italian mobsters in Montreal. "I guess he knew the Cottroni people. They're not generally good names to mention. He was not hanging around with them, but the local Mafia was running most of the nightclubs in Montreal. If you did a lot of nightclub reporting you got to know these people. Naturally, you wanna be on their good sides, not only for the fact that they owned the nightclubs, but for the fact that you could get a lot of free drinks.

"And a lot of free news."

Mike James, an ex-employee of Azaria's, recalled those days with enthusiasm, "You'd basically deal with the crime and gore—crimes based on truth. They sell 'em in supermarkets now and the supermarkets don't like it, so [today] they do a lot of celebs and they do a lot of UFOs and they don't do any more major fucky-fuck and no more major 'Pop's Head Cut Off,' but they used to. No more crazed dwarf stories. Now it's 'Herve Villechaize's Love Secrets.' "

James said in the four years he worked there, writing under a variety of names, he remembered the *Examiner* as "really fuckin' cheapo and sleazy. The version today is a very high-class version. We dealt in severed limbs and dead baby soup stories—that's what we called 'em—a particular kind of story, you know? So and so digs up mom's head . . . 'I'm a slut, a complete slut!' or the overline would read that she screams at cops as she throws out human head, 'IT'S MY MOM!' in 244-point type, y'know? 'Junkyard Dog Digs Up Head.'

"Azaria was a great man for fucking secretaries," James said. "Vader said the man would get pimples if he didn't fuck once a day." (Vader said he doesn't recall saying anything like this specifically but acknowledged, "I could have said something like that.") James described Azaria's unbridled libido breaking out during a meeting. The publisher "suddenly grabbed a blanket and put it over a secretary's head and they go on humping and there's this noise, this mutual gasping, and the rest just went on with their meeting."

James recalled how the *Globe* ended up in Florida: "I worked at *Globe* while I was at the law school there at McGill University. I worked for Johnny Vader for a while—that was before the *Sun*—and the reason they moved to Florida was because they had tremendous union problems. The Newspaper Guild Local 222 came in and organized the whole fuckin' newsroom, so they moved everybody out to Florida overnight. God, they threw 70 people out of work like that! Rosenbloom and his partners."

Greetings from Tabloid Valley

The Globe Communications tabloid empire is still in Palm Beach County with American Media's papers. It shifted operations in 1982 to escape impending unionization. Rosenbloom had considered moving to New York or California, but Florida's employer-favorable laws and proximity to a pool of chronically unemployed tabloid types made South Florida the ideal place to continue his line of money-making publications.

Rosenbloom, in contrast to Pope, is a retiring man. He rarely shows his face at the Boca Raton headquarters and when he does, it is to confer with his minions in their plush, garishly decorated offices on the building's third floor. In front of the headquarters is a bronzed statue of Atlas holding aloft an enormous globe.

Most of his employees have rarely, if ever, seen the man—and then only at the company Christmas party. Although he (and sometimes his wife) will exert explicit editorial control over the paper, he doesn't come down to the second-floor newsroom and confer with anyone. Instructions are likely to arrive by phone, written message, or from an editor summoned to the upstair's offices. He doesn't like to give interviews and doesn't try to create any mystique about himself. Which is, of course, the Rosenbloom mystique.

Over the years, Rosenbloom is said to have doled out small pieces of the business, but retains the lion's share of the corporation and power. Under his direction, Globe will not reveal profit or sales figures to anyone, and it isn't known for sure if either Azaria or anyone else owns part of the enterprise.

And if Rosenbloom's empire lacks the explicit Mob contacts and flamboyant behavior of Pope's publications, it still fosters the cutthroat office politics and bizarre behavior typical of the tabloids' employees. Nothing demonstrates the capricious power Rosenbloom has than the dynamics between his family and editors.

Selig Adler was a rising star in the company during the 1970s while he was an editor for a Rosenbloom publication in New York City. Rosenbloom's secretary, the comely Bernadette, was getting on the man's nerves, trying to tell Adler how to edit. Adler put her in her place, calling her a "dumb cunt."

Unfortunately for Adler, Rosenbloom was in the middle of divorcing his wife to legitimize the affair he was carrying on with Bernadette. From then on, Adler languished in dead-end positions. Years later and a $20 million divorce from Bernadette changed Old Rosie's mind, and Selig was brought back from the bushes to resume editorship of another of Rosenbloom's magazine's—the short-lived *People* look-alike called *US*.

When Rosie's current wife, Valerie, found out the *Examiner* was doing a story titled "Mistresses: How They Destroy Your Marriage," she ordered editor Billy Burt to change the focus. Burt ordered the story rewritten according to Mrs. Rosenbloom's instructions, which were written in the margins of the original draft. She changed everything—names, quotes, places—all to support her new headline: "Mistresses Can Make a Marriage Stronger."

Having been a mistress herself, it was theorized, she couldn't abide by the idea that such people were homewreckers. The issue was *not* a success with housewives at the checkout line.

Other family members are in on the act, too. Rosenbloom's two "retarded sons" (as one ex-editor described them) have various duties within the company, but are considered to be less than brilliant businessmen or journalists. It is rumored even Rosenbloom's teenaged daughters have had a hand in deciding what goes on the cover of the *National Examiner*, something that would not be tolerated at either the *Globe* (way too much money at stake) or the *Sun* (edited by Azaria's original partner, John Vader).

Vader is constantly rumored to have either ownership of a chunk of Globe Communications or an iron-clad "no-fire" clause in his contract. Vader denies both of these things, but does admit he and Azaria had "an agreement." He won't specify what it was, but he said he once "took care" of the business for a while and implied he still derives some kind of benefit from it. Vader is well-liked by everyone at Globe and it is impossible to think of the organization without him.

While American Media consolidated its power, Maxwell bid to purchase all three of Globe Communication's supermarket tabloids (*National Examiner, Globe* and *Sun*) in 1990. This is curious since the three tabloids were experiencing a steady decline in circulation at the time and were not expected to improve. Clearly Maxwell was not looking for easy money. With hindsight it seems probable that Maxwell, like his "rival" Murdoch and others who seek to control media, was interested in the papers for propaganda purposes. (Maxwell was exposed as an Israeli spy well before his mysterious death.)

The reclusive Mike Rosenbloom, who controls the privately owned Globe Corporation, decided $300+ million offered by Maxwell was not enough to buy his collection of failing and inconsequential tabloids.

Why Southern Florida?

Lots of people know that the tabloid headquarters are in Palm Beach County in southern Florida. Fewer people know why. Although that area is called "Tabloid Valley," it isn't a valley at all. This chunk of the state is flat scrubland on the edge of the Everglades. It is hot and muggy except in winter, and it isn't close to anything—one reason it became a popular vacation spot and criminal hideout.

The following short history of southeast Florida, the Mob, the CIA and the tabloids is not to suggest that Costello, Lansky, Kennedy, or, especially, Generoso Pope were agents for Israel, terrorist organizations, or any other foreign country. Primarily these guys were businessmen, but they also had certain political philosophies and never hid them. For instance, in the 1950s Lansky was better known for his overseas involvement in Cuba than anywhere else. Later on he became far more interested in Zionism than in his gangster businesses.

By the time Gene Pope stepped into the world of espionage, the underworld held many parts of South Florida in its grip. Generoso Pope, his close friends Frank Costello and Roy Cohn, and Costello's business partners Joe Kennedy and Meyer Lansky were well-acquainted with this obscure stretch of beach.

The Mob influence in this region counters the "official" stories of Generoso Pope's presence in Florida—that he moved the *Enquirer* offices there in 1971 either at the behest of his wife (who fell in love with the area while on vacation), or because Pope wanted to take advantage of the region's supposedly lower taxes. Moving a celebrity tabloid to South Florida made as much sense as moving the paper to a small town in South Dakota. Pope had friends in the area. Pope never mentioned them when explaining the move.

Outsiders' Guide to South Florida

In the 1920s South Florida was nearly as wild as the Western frontier 50 years earlier. Few people wanted to live year-round in such a bestial climate, plagued by hurricanes and mosquitoes. It was home to Bible-toting religious fanatics, migrant workers, dirt farmers, impoverished fishers and even some Seminoles who had not yet been subdued by the U.S. Cavalry. This chunk of America, sticking off the continent like an appendix, was treated much much the same. As long as it didn't cause pain, people didn't care what happened to it. That it should host the publishers of all six supermarket tabloids doesn't seem natural, except if one knows who did migrate to this part of Florida.

In 1926 a hurricane pounded Florida's Atlantic Coast from Coral Gables to Boca Raton, destroying what little there was in the way of cinder-block houses and wooden shacks. As it entered the 1930s, Florida was an uncomfortable place full of outlaws. Perhaps its main attraction was a stunning lack of law enforcement or even government. Breakaway sects from unorthodox religions came to Florida and set up utopian communes. On the Gulf Coast, mad scientists started building a miles-long apparatus to try to prove the Earth was really a hollow sphere and that China could be reached through the clouds. Florida was a no-man's-land where you could go if you had used up all your cards somewhere else, or if you wanted to start something on your own.

One of the first ambitious gangsters to arrive from the north was Chicagoan "Potatoes" Kaufman. He hooked up with a Broward County bookmaker named Frank Shireman and set up a gambling establishment in the mid-'30s. Kaufman specialized in a casino-type betting establishment based on horse-racing results, which came in over a wire into a weather-beaten shack ostentatiously called "The Plantations." It did pretty well. There was no competition.

Potatoes was joined by Jimmy "Blue Eyes" Alo, a friend and partner of "Lucky" Luciano, who also sent down his close associate Meyer Lansky to supervise a merger deal the two gangsters proposed to Potatoes.

First they had to take care of the pesky town fathers who were harassing the Plantations and threatening to close it down. Lansky took a two-pronged approach. He purchased several adjacent parcels of land, and whenever a gambling injunction was ordered against the betting establishment, the place was moved to a neighboring lot. He also started handing out money to more than two dozen local organizations. The Elks Club got a nice chunk of money, as did the Fort Lauderdale Shriners, the Hollywood Fishing Tournament and the South Florida Children's Hospital. When Lansky opened a more permanent version of the Plantation in 1936, there were no more complaints. The Plantation soon boasted carpeting and one of the finest kitchens in the country.

With its newly established gaming industry, this section of South Florida flourished and turned into a little Las Vegas. Where in 1929 there had been only a dozen or so hotels in Miami Beach, by 1939 there were several hundred. Many hotel guests would arrive in taxis and limos to the Plantations, where they enjoyed big-name entertainment. A dog track opened in '36 in Hollywood, Florida, and another in Hallandale in '39.

The county did have law enforcement, though. Corrupt county officials simply doubled their fines and penalties, and by the late-'40s bribery and extortion had become a big ritual. Gamblers would be hauled in for "disorderly conduct," then forfeit bond when they didn't show up for court. Everybody was happy.

Lansky was so happy that he expanded his gambling operations to Cuba in 1938, where Batista had taken over five years earlier. Lansky maintained his ties with Luciano, especially during WWII when the

U.S. government turned to Luciano and other Mafiosi to help them police the docks of the eastern seaboard and later to invade Sicily.

Back in NYC

Meanwhile, Pope's pal Frank Costello had become "King of the Slots" in New York. He ran into a snag when crime-busting Mayor La Guardia seized some of Frank's slot machines, put them on a barge and dumped them into the harbor. Costello relocated a lot of his business to Louisiana where another mobster, Sam Giancana, was in charge. Costello never left New York entirely, but he was hounded there.

During Prohibition Costello formed a loose partnership with Joe Kennedy of Boston, who later moved to New York City, too. Costello told author Peter Maas he "helped Kennedy get rich." Another mafioso, "Doc" Stacher, who was in exile in Israel running from IRS charges, confirmed to Israeli reporters that Costello and Kennedy were once business partners but that the two had had a falling out.

Costello at one time controlled Tammany Hall—the political machine that held sway over New York City politics for many years. Costello frequently backed state judges—a matter brought up during the famous Kefauver hearings in the early 1950s. It was acknowledged that Costello had at least once sought to set up a judge but had sworn off the practice when he got his "hands burnt."

Nevertheless, Costello seems to have played key roles with not only other judges, but political appointees of every kind. Roy Cohn said in his memoirs that it was Frank Costello who got Irving Saypol his job as U.S. attorney by using his Tammany Hall connections and association with Carmine DeSapio. (Later Saypol would achieve notoriety during the Rosenberg trials.)

As luck would have it, in the fall of 1945 reform candidate DeLesseps Morrison was elected mayor of New Orleans partially on his promise to rid the city of the Costello–Lansky combine. Time for Costello to move on again. So Lansky brought Costello to Florida.

Mafia's Policing During the War

A 1993 *Vanity Fair* exposé on J. Edgar Hoover and his dealings with the Mafia suggests that in 1939 Costello helped Hoover make his famous bust of Louis "Lepke" Buchalter while Lepke was head of "Murder Inc." In return for his help, the imprisoned "Lucky Luciano" (who had approved the handing over of Lepke) was promised some relief. In the end, Lepke got the chair and Luciano went free—but not before he and Lansky did a little work for the U.S. government's fledgling spy agency, the OSS.

During World War II, Luciano and the Mafia were in a position to help the government. In the first three months of the war following the attack on Pearl Harbor, the United States lost more than 120 merchant ships to German subs that seemed to come and go with impunity. Not a single U-boat was sunk. When the French liner *Normandie* caught fire while being converted to a high-speed troop ship, military intelligence began to suspect infiltration. To combat the problem, it turned to the organization that controlled the docks all along the East Coast. The Mafia helped the U.S. Navy police the docks all the way down to Florida, where they oversaw the off-loading of produce from the United Fruit Company. The Mafia more or less sold the Navy "insurance" from sabotage.

At the same time, a gangster–intelligence group known as "B-3" operated out of Hotel Fourteen above New York's Copacabana. The imprisoned Luciano directed its activities, aided by Meyer Lansky, who personally relayed his messages. In 1946, the government repaid Luciano's wartime assistance by releasing him from jail and sending him home to Italy. Luciano was accompanied to the docks by both Lansky and Costello.

Post-War Entanglements

After the war things continued as normal in South Florida. Lansky's clubs became plusher and the talent better and more famous. Both Jimmy Durante and Frank Sinatra got their starts in these clubs. Just a few miles north, in Palm Beach, Joe Kennedy relaxed in what would come to be the family "compound" made so famous in the 1991 rape trial.

It was prosperity for all. When Golda Meir visited the area in 1946 and 1947, Lansky's gambling house gave her a donation for her terrorist group, Haganah. Lansky went further in his aid to Israel, reviving his B-3 contacts at the Hotel Fourteen and transforming it into a base for Israeli agents who were trying to illegally purchase American arms. At that time Israel was still Palestine and under the control of Great Britain, and Jewish militant groups like the Haganah were being sought after and executed as terrorists.

While Lansky's reconstituted B-3 group looked for weapons to supply the Jewish colonials in Israel, it also did what it could to hamper the supply of American weapons to Arab countries. When Haganah agents gave Lansky the name of a Pittsburgh arms dealer they knew was arranging shipments to Arabs through the New York-New Jersey waterfront, Lansky told them, "I'm at your service."

Part of the Pittsburgh consignment soon fell overboard, while the rest of it got "accidentally" loaded on ships bound for Israel. One agent connected with Lansky was Johnny "Cockeye" Dunn, who was later convicted of waterfront enforcement murder and condemned to death in 1949.

When Fidel Castro took over Cuba in 1959—in many ways the southern arm of the Florida Mafia's gambling operations—few people were closer to the local economy, and people, as Lansky and his friends. Surprisingly, Lansky's casinos continued to operate for a short time after the revolution, and Lansky vocally backed the Castro regime. Eventually, however, his gambling houses and swank hotels were seized and de-glitzed, and Lansky was thrown out of the country. The Mafia was then hired by the U.S. government to retake Cuba. Soon, South Florida became home to boatloads of fleeing Cubans and nascent Bay of Pigs' armies.

Mafia–CIA connections in regard to Cuba are clearly documented. The events that follow lead toward the eventual assassination of JFK.

The numerous conspiracy theories related to JFK's death do not seem to concern Generoso Pope or any tabloid directly. However, the tabloids have been used from the very beginning to fuel a national obsession with JFK and a hatred of Communism and, especially, of Cuba and Castro.

Castro has served as a staple tabloid "bad guy" since he took power. Stories about him have been concocted almost since the day he took power. As late as the spring of 1992, Castro was reported by the *Sun* to have instigated, then personally taken part in, the riots that broke out in L.A. after the Rodney King verdict. Doctored cover photos showed Castro kicking in a store window as part of a mob.

Pope's Cozy Relationships in His Hometown

Following the lead of others who did business in South Florida, Pope knew what he had to do to succeed. The Christmas tree was just his first and most ostentatious bribe. Over the years Pope donated millions of dollars to charity groups, police departments, and other civic institutions. He donated $5 million to the JFK Memorial Hospital, where he also served as chairman of the board of trustees. Each year the police and fire departments would present Mr. Pope with a wish list of equipment they would like for their forces. Generally, he bought everything on the list.

Still, despite the "I LUV the *ENQUIRER*" attitude, Lantana has never been a "company town" in the real sense. Pope did not provide a lot of *Enquirer* jobs for the locals, but he greased the palms of those who had power. Like Lansky before him, he knew what it took to get things done and recognized the necessity of this kind of community bribery. Lantana could have lived pretty well without the *Enquirer*, but why should it?

Over at the *Enquirer*, Pope's dictums live on mostly as anecdotes, and the acronym *PGP* ("Passed Generoso Pope") is still scribbled on a story OK'd for publication. Now that Pope is gone it's probably all right to write about the CIA, the Mafia or Sophia Loren.

◆ ◆ ◆

Appendix A

Tracking Down Back Issues

U p to this point, only folklorists have bothered to examine the content and history of the tabs. To tabloid scholars, lack of access to back issues is a constant problem. True ephemera, supermarket tabloids have not been seriously collected by any library, and tabloids either restrict access to back issues or deny they have them. Much of the tabloids' running commentary on American society is lost to history. Anyone wishing to study tabloids in general or themes like the Bermuda Triangle or Bigfoot had to content themselves with scraps of tabs pulled from piles of trash.

The *Enquirer* claims not to have saved any copies prior to 1967, which is hard to believe since it sometimes refers to earlier editions. At Globe Communications, access to the company library is restricted among the staff, who must log past issues and other material in and out and keep it at their desks. They can be fired for leaving the building with so much as a clipping. Needless to say, the general public is not allowed to browse the stacks.

Most back issues of tabloids are held in small, private collections, and not even the Library of Congress has a good collection. However, deep within the New York Public Library is rumored to be microfilmed back issues of the *National Enquirer* and perhaps other tabloids, but getting to them requires permission.

Most studies of supermarket tabloids are forced to take a random sample of tab content covering a week to, at most, a year. Other studies have to rely on the odd copy that comes available through serendipitous means. Liz Bird, author of *For Enquiring Minds*, flew to Texas to read back issues of the *National Enquirer* held by an old woman. She had kept the ancient copies not because she was a tabloid fan, but because they formed part of her compulsive collection of JFK memorabilia.

Studies using a random week's tabloid output find standard themes and topics. Globe Communications' confidential study of the best-selling covers for all six tabloids from 1979 to 1986 shows regular patterns. Liz Taylor, amazing diets, and secret shames of various Hollywood personalities are staples. This study lists only the contents of issues deemed successful in terms of sales. Duds do not appear here, and there's no way to know if Liz Taylor is "sure-fire" or not since no low-selling papers are listed.

This study showed that the two "wacky" tabs, the *Weekly World News* and the *Sun*, do not often have terribly successful issues and probably sell at a very regular rate. Occasionally, one or both of these publications is listed, but a trend is impossible to discern from this study.

Breaks with tradition, such as the *Examiner*'s decision to run stories about Jim Bakker's downfall, won't show up in localized studies. For this reason, tabs must be collected for research purposes. Big changes, like the elimination of gore from tabloids wishing to enter the supermarket checkout lines, have been noted in mainstream publications. Still, the only way to truly scrutinize the tabs is to archive the issues, which is just starting to be done, most notably by the Department of Popular Culture at Bowling Green University, in Bowling Green, Ohio.

Deep within its bowels, the Library of Congress has a lot of back issues of tabloids. However, since the library depends on the publications to send in issues to be archived, it is missing most issues of most tabs.

At the Library of Congress, the card number for the *National Enquirer* is 87-92669 h term and the call number for the microfilm is (o) 83/146. These are the same call numbers needed to find the

Enquirer at the Los Angeles Public Library, Sacramento Public Library and Long Beach Public Library. However, these last three libraries may not have complete collections.

The *Weekly World News* is also at the Los Angeles Public Library, which has the past six months (before they are presumably trashed). Copies of the *WWN* as of 1979 are at the Library of Congress, but the library does not list its holdings.

Perhaps the largest collection of tabloids—mainly copies of the *National Enquirer*—is buried in the research libraries of the New York Public Library system. To get at these print and microfilmed issues, you practically have to know someone, as the material is kept locked up and reserved for scholars. Casual calls to the library will give the erroneous information that back issues of the tabs don't exist. Anyone interested in looking through these archives would do well to have the call numbers and other information on hand.

At the New York Public Library, the *National Enquirer* can be found under *ZAN 9151B and *ZY in room 315 at the end of the North Hall. There you can find issues 1957–1959. The paper may also be filed under *ZY along with issues from 1959–1962 and from 1962–1973.

Issues of the *National Enquirer* and the *Star* as of 12 January 1993 are in the Periodicals Room of the New York Public Library.

Collections of the *National Examiner*, the *Globe* and the *Sun* aren't found through the interlibrary loan lists OCLC and RLIN. They can be found only in specialized research libraries such as those maintained by the tabs. As for tab libraries, you can forget it. Neither one allows any of the public into them, and the *Enquirer* even claims that neither it nor any other library has pre-1967 issues in its collection—something we know isn't true.

Any researcher interested in doing a thorough study of the tabloids throughout their entire histories would do well to either secure the cooperation of the tabs themselves, or else be prepared to spend thousands of hours poring through brittle rolls of microfilm.

◆ ◆ ◆

Appendix B

Interoffice Memos and Notes from the Field

The following pages are examples of interoffice memos dictating the desired tabloid writing styles.

The first 4-page memo was sent in an attempt to get the writing staff to interject more emotion and "color" into the stories. The second 4-page memo concerns the subtleties of interviewing celebrities. It's clear from reading that the tabs are well-practiced in avoiding lawsuits and protecting themselves if one arises. Finally, a 3-page collection of notes on the suicide of Kurt Cobain details the pursuit of a celebrity story.

The thoroughness of the memos reveals a great deal of careful thought. The tabs never make an uncalculated move.

M E M O R A N D U M

TO: Editorial Staff   DATE: August 17, 1973

FROM:

From now on ENQUIRER stories should be packed with color and emotion. This will take extra effort from everyone--reporters, article editors, writers and editors.

Our stories must make our readers react. We should touch our readers' souls...cause them to smile, to get lumps in their throats, to break down and cry. We want The ENQUIRER filled with stories like the classic "Yes, Virginia, there is a Santa Claus" which has outlived both its author and the little girl who inspired it.

EMOTION

How do we get more emotion into our stories? The job starts with the reporter. The first step is to study your assignment and think of all the ways that emotions can be used in it. Mentally frame up the kind of moving, provocative quotes that will be needed to get a reader--a live human being--to cry real tears, to smile or burst out laughing. Firmly fix in your mind your story's angle and think about the kind of facts and quotes that will be needed to write an ENQUIRER story. Plan your interview. Determine the course you'll follow.

Most of the emotional impact a reporter will provide in a story will be in quotes. Talk to all the people involved. Not just the hero, but the person rescued, the witnesses, the ambulance driver, the doctor, the cops--find out what they can remember. Search about and find the people who can supply extra punch.

We need quotes that tug at the heart. Remember the story of the two orphans who inspired Father Flannagan, the founder of Boys' Town. One ragged little fellow was struggling along, carrying another boy who was too tired to walk. When the priest asked if he could help, the older boy said: "He ain't heavy, Father...he's my brother."

Prod, push and probe the main characters in the story. Help them frame their answers. For example: How did it feel? Bad. No, I mean what did it feel like? I don't know, it just hurt. Was it a sharp pain? No. Was it more like a toothache? No. Have you ever felt anything like it before? Not really, but it was something like an electrical shock. Where did you feel it? It hit me in the back of the neck and went down my spine. Did you scream? I couldn't. Let's see if I've got this straight. You said, "The pain hit me. It was like an electrical shock that started in my neck and shot down my spine. I wanted to scream but I couldn't. I've never felt anything like it". Yes, that's it.

Ask leading questions. "Do you ever go into the corner and cry?" What do you pray for?" Has God forsaken you?"

If the person is articulate, listen and record what's said carefully. Sharp quotes--in the exact language of the way the person actually talks--are often the meat of the story.

Writing Memo, page 2 of 4 pages ...

If he says: "Never has so much been owed by so many to so few", don't change it to "we owe a lot to the RAF".

Or if he says: "I don't want to make a big deal out of it, but if I have to, I'll die for my country" don't make it "One must always be on one's guard to avoid exaggeration" but I'm quite prepared to make the supreme sacrifice".

Quotes should not only be appropriate but believable. A Japanese carpenter should not sound like Ernest Hemingway, or vice versa.

When shooting for emotional quotes think about the things that affect you. We all admire courage but dislike bragging. Make a hero's quote reflect modesty, quiet determination, a sense of duty. Let others apply the praise. The witness said, "It was unbelievable. The most heroic act I've ever seen" but the hero says, "I just did what any father would do".

Appeals need the same treatment. No one has much sympathy for the person with his hand out, but people are willing to dig in for someone who is trying but who just can't cope with the overwhelming odds. Don't have the persons ask for things...get them to tell the reader their dreams and their hopes. For example, don't say, "We're broke and we need money to buy a house in a better neighborhood". Say, "My dream is that someday we'll be able to get out of this rat hole and give Ricky a clean, warm bed...He's never asked for much... he deserves to die with a little dignity."

Most people are fond of kids and animals. Kids or animals in trouble produce very deep emotional reactions in readers.

Constantly think of the readers. If you were reading the story, what would affect you? This goes for writers and editors as well.

Work to get a telling quote that backs up the main angle of the story. This especially is needed in "miracle cures" and occult stories. A direct quote is the best back up and when the writers have one to work with it saves time and space which can be used to develop color and emotion in the finished story.

The writer's first job is to read and evaluate the file to determine if it contains the story the check-in sheet promised and if there is enough good material to write the kind of colorful and emotional pieces we want.

Stories that have emotional impact have to be carefully crafted. It doesn't work just to shovel in a lot of emotional quotes. The story must have pace and tone. It cannot be all fireworks and sparkle. The story must have a framework of facts. The writer must clearly determine what his story is about, what points it must cover, what facts it must convey. Then the job is to weave emotion and color with the facts to tell the story in a compelling and interesting way.

The story cannot be all emotions, all high points. You need passages that stand in relief of the high points. You set the reader up and then smash! You hit him in the pit of the stomach. In the right context and in the proper setting, just a simple word such as "yes" can have a powerful impact.

Writers should try to milk the files and rewrite and polish stories to get as much of the emotional material in as they can. But remember, the story must have pace. Ups and downs, highs and lows to play off each other.

Use lots of quotes and select ones that bring the person to life. It's best to avoid writing in dialects or unusual vernacular such as Brooklyneese, or hippie talk. If your story calls for portraying a person as a colorful character, use dialect devices sparingly. Too much makes it difficult to read and understand.

However, if the person has a colorful and unusual way of putting things and says things such as "I'm as weary as a politician's promise," capture that flavor in his quotes.

Copy editors should be alert to the problems of establishing tone and pace in an emotional story...particularly when making cuts. Too lean and you lose the sheen.

This goes for changing quotes. Take the story about the mother who had the flag that covered her son's coffin stolen. The writer wrote: "I wish they'd bring it back...God how I wish they'd bring it back." But it was changed to "If they don't bring it back, God help them."

The same goes for inserting left out facts. Pick a spot where they don't get in the way of the emotional material.

Who needs: "Mom, I can't tell you how good it feels to be home again in West Chester, Ohio, a small community 25 miles south of Cleveland." Make your editing improve the story. Cut the clutter, select a better synonym and insert those dots...and dashes--where they do the most good. Sometimes the best job an editor can do is to bounce the story back for a rewrite.

COLOR

Many of the things said about getting emotion into our stories also applies to getting color in. Again, it requires cooperation from everyone.

One of the chief purposes of color in an ENQUIRER story is to make it unmistakably clear to the reader that our man was there on the scene. The reporter should collect plenty of specific details about the place. No vague things that can be faked like she had on a white dress and sat in a chair on her large patio. Better to say: She was dressed all in white, white shoes, a crisp white tennis dress and a white hat with a big circular brim that flopped down around on all sides. She sat sedately in one of four white ice-cream parlor chairs placed around a white circular table. The patio was 75 feet square and the rough cement surface was also bleached white. It was 9 A.M., the sun was bright and I had to squint to take in the shimmering scene. The green stripes on the table's umbrella leaped out in contrast.

The writer may not use all that great stuff but he's got a lot better idea what the scene was like if he needs it for the story.

Search for telling details that either reflect the expected picture, (the old sea captain's home is full of charts and knot boards and nautical knicknacks) or that provide an unexpected contrast. (The chorus girl with the classical record collection).

Get specific. Jot down the size of things, note the brand of pipe tobacco. Paint a word picture of the person. Tell what he looks like, give the statistics but also let us know if he has a nervous habit of constantly touching the bridge of his glasses.

If getting there was a problem, tell us about it.

The writer has the job of selecting. You won't be able to use all the color provided. You'll have to pick and this means some good things won't make it. Remember you've still got a story to tell and the color is sprinkled in to make the story more interesting. You're not writing just to get in a lot of colorful material. Pick the stuff that best emphasizes the point you're trying to make or the stuff that offers the best contrast and relief. Select a few things that bring the people in the story to life. But don't overdo a good thing.

Copy editors will have to help here. If you read the writer's version first, any excess should be apparent. Personal preferences are sure to arise and let's all try to resolve our personal likes and dislikes in a way that works out best for the story and the paper.

There should be some exciting and interesting times ahead for us all.

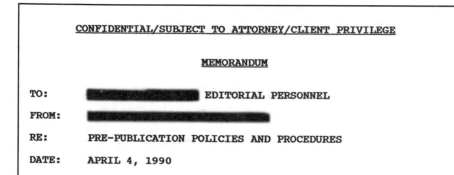

MEMORANDUM

TO: ███████████████ EDITORIAL PERSONNEL

FROM: ████████████████████

RE: PRE-PUBLICATION POLICIES AND PROCEDURES

DATE: APRIL 4, 1990

Celebrity Stories

Special care must be taken in handling celebrity stories. We have avoided major pitfalls in this area by being discriminate as to our sources and by avoiding muckraking or harshly negative angles. This is not to say, however, that we will not print contentious stories; we will do so if we can support the story with reliable and credible sources. Several criteria are applicable:

1. Know your source. This is particularly important for stories that are contentious. Sources must be known and identified! You must be able to rely on the credibility of your source, and such reliance must be well placed. If you are at all dubious as to the credibility of your source, verify the story through a further source. If such further source is not available, the story cannot be published. An individual who is not well known to you and of proven reliability must not be used as a principal source for a contentious or negative story.

2. Always use our own library to verify as much background information as possible. The clips or source material that are used as backup should then be included or noted in the story file.

3. Never use a headline or imply in a story introduction that the celebrity has given a personal interview if that not be the case. This situation is fraught with danger and should be avoided. Make clear in the body of the story that the celebrity "revealed to the Daily News" or "tearfully confessed to the Medical Post".

4. Keep all tapes and notes in the story files. While the optimum is to tape each celebrity interview, it is

understood that this cannot realistically be done in every case. If taping is not feasible, detailed notes must be taken. The tapes and/or notes must be placed in the files with any clips used for background information. All too often both tapes and notes have proven to be unavailable when requested.

5. Avoid slipshod, indifferent or careless reporting. Whenever a statement could injure someone's reputation or have a potentially negative effect, treat it with due regard for its probable impact. Facts of every story should be confirmed and verified, in accordance with customary professional procedures.

6. Truth is a defense, but there is a vast difference between what <u>is</u> true and what can be <u>proved</u> to be true to a jury. If any doubt whatsoever exists as to whether a story is accurate further support must be obtained. Bear in mind, a retraction is not a defense to a libel action but serves merely to mitigate or lessen damages.

7. There is no such thing as a "false opinion," so greater latitude exists with expressions of opinion than with statements of fact. Comment or criticism must be based on facts that are fully stated and accurate, and must indicate that the statements are intended as such, i.e. editorials, reviews, columns. What constitutes legally defined "opinion" can be a difficult question - ask.

8. Try to get "the other side of the story." Always attempt to contact a story subject even if you anticipate a "No comment." A description of such attempt must be made a part of the story.

9. Particular care must be taken with quotes. The fact that a source is quoted accurately is not necessarily a defense to a libel action if we have reason to believe the quoted statement contains false information.

10. In cases of private persons or non-celebrities, be sensitive to cases that may involve the invasion of one's privacy. A lack of concern as to the sensitive and/or non-newsworthy elements of a private person's life may only earn the Publication the wrath of a jury.

<u>Lead Sheets</u>

It is imperative that a lead sheet is completed for each and every story. A copy of the lead sheet that must be used for each story is attached. The appropriate section of the lead sheet should contain the following information for each source:

-2-

1. Name.

2. Relationship to subject of story.

3. Date and time interviewed.

4. Circumstances of interview. If the interview was done on the phone, include the source's phone number. If it was done in person, record the location (with address if applicable) and the names of others present.

5. Record whether the source's statements were transcribed in notes or on tape, and where the notes and/or tape can be located.

6. Each source should be labeled with a letter and that letter should be entered in the margin of the copy next to the information supplied by that source. Writers should transfer these letters to the appropriate place in the margins of the rewritten version of the story.

Rewriting

Frequently a story or clip comes across the desk which the reporter wishes to use, or to incorporate into a story. It is permissible to rewrite the clip or story with several caveats:

1. It is never permissible to take the story verbatim from another source.

2. Use your own experience, research and creativity to interject your unique style into the clip.

3. Use the telephone for verifying the facts in the clip and for researching new facts about a story. This is particularly important for major stories, for stories that may be contentious or in cases when you simply do not have enough information. This is not required for all stories; use your professional judgment; the uniqueness, importance and prominence of a story are some of the relevant criteria.

4. Rewrite judiciously. For example, in many clips there are what might be termed "giveaway" phrases or quotes which must be disguised. If the original author or agency copy uses particularly flowery adjectives or descriptive color passages, then you must avoid such language and substitute your own creativity. A "giveaway" quote can be circumvented by using it in the third person, or by attributing it as "told a European magazine".

5. Be alert and sensitive to the "routine" story of seemingly minor significance. If such stories do not get appropriate

editorial attention, the result can be a disproportionate amount of litigation. Make reports of arrests, investigations and other judicial or legislative proceedings and records precise and accurate.

6. Edit all stories carefully to make certain they state precisely what you want to say. Do not use sly or cute innuendo to suggest some misbehavior that you do not intend to describe explicitly. If a story may injure one's reputation, be circumspect.

7. Study the lead sheet. There have been instances when the thrust of the story follows the introduction of the source clip instead of the lead sheet introduction. Our policy is to follow the suggested angle on the lead sheet, not from the source clip. Make every effort to follow our own suggested angle unless, of course, you can properly create a better and stronger angle of your own.

8. Study the clip. Usually by looking at a clip you can determine the extent you can go with a story. Professional rewriting can always improve on and disguise any agency and staff-written daily newspaper stories. Be alert for copyright stories (some of them we cannot handle as straight rewrites), syndicated stories, and one-shot exclusives by big-name by-lines. These are be fraught with problems, and we should discuss our approach to these as they arise.

Photos

Selecting file photos to accompany stories can always be a hazard. Simple guidelines here, however, are:

1. Always read the captions on pictures. Pictures pertaining to unrelated stories should never even be considered.

2. Make certain that the person or scene depicted in the pictures has not been edited out of the story. Also make sure it pertains to the thrust of the story (i.e. a key quote) and has not somehow been edited from the story.

3. If a suitable picture is not available from agencies or our own files, don't take a risk with an alternative from a doubtful source. Set up our own simulated or model shoot, although we must make reference to the reconstruction in the cutline.

4. A former Hell's Angel rider and wife successfully sued a daily paper which had used a file picture of them from their hell-raising Hell's Angel's days. They were just two people in a group shot of fearless toughs which accompanied

-4-

Session View - noomail

[Navigator: Sending message about "attention Brian"]

To: >FAX: 1-914-332-5043
Subject: attention Brian

Dear Marvanne and Brian,

Here are the facts I gathered on Kurt Cobain's suicide along with some rumors and opinions from
people who are in a position to know. Luckily I know some people in town who are real plugged
into the music and art scenes here -- I am not. Although Cobain was famous and hung out in
public places, he really lived in a kind of demi-monde here.

In the first hours after he was found on Friday, it was a lot easier to get people to talk than
later on as people clammed up either out of grief, fatigue or orders from superior⌐   ⌐ow nobody

is talking.

One of my sources is/was a reporter at a city newspaper whose wife is friend   ⌐ ife of
the cop who arrived 2nd on the scene. His first name is Fenton -- I don't k   name.
Fenton told his wife something about what was in the note and he is the one w   ⌐⌐ographed it
for the police.

According to this source (the reporter repeating what her friend repeated from her husband) the
letter was long. I got the impression it was more than one page. Other people had that
impression, too but the newspapers the next day were adamant that it was a single page.
Somehow the cop came home with the impression that Cobain had considered suicide "for days".
I'm not clear whether or not he got that from the letter.

Most importantly he said the letter indicated that Kurt Cobain's wife, Courtney Love, AND his
band had "abandoned" him.

This is probably the most important thing I found out since the reporter was not a Kurt Cobain
fan and didn't follow any of his life. I doubt that the cop and the wives knew much about
Cobain, either. But I do believe this same cop had been out to the place before within the
previous week.

This morning I was told by a friend in Portland, OR that he had heard a rumor that
" Courtney was threatening to leave him."

That source is a good one, he is friends with a lot of people in the same circles as Cobain. He

also told me:

"A guy in Portland who was close to him is a fellow named "Thor," who runs Tim
Kerr records. They did the recording of Kurt doing guitar noise behind
William Burroughs vocalizing. Thor scored a lot of heroin for Cobain."

he also told me:

"Cobain's favorite band and close friends, The Melvins, were busted at
Portland airport four or five months ago for carrying or selling heroin. I
believe that they got probation. Strangely enough, one of the Melvins to get
busted (and later kicked out of the band) was Shirley Temple Black's
daughter. Don't remember her name."

AND

"Kurt was a gun nut. Hated his mother."

When I asked him for some clarification he said.

"Everything I hear about Cobain is gossip. I have no absolute through lines.

4/30/94 19:32   Page 1

Session View - noomail

TK records is a local label in town. I don't know Thor, but know people who
know of him. Thor was reputedly distraught over the suicide, considered
himself a friend. Don't use me as a reference.

"The Melvins bust was reported by a tab several months ago on the Shirley
Temple daughter angle. (A friend of mine was busted there as well.)"

This guy is a good source and doesn't want to be named or cited. He's a publisher from L.A. who

has been in on the fringe of culture for years and years — also in music. Cobain and other
Nirvana members lived in L.A. until pretty recently.

An acquaintance of mine, Melissa Rossi, was hired by Newsweek and Esquire to report on the
suicide has been interviewing *everybody* (she has all the best connections) did not seem to
have any good or juicy information as of Sunday am when she filed for Newsweek. Also I have it
on good authority that she has not heard what I heard about the contents of the letter, namely
that Courtney Love had left Cobain.

OTHER POSSIBLE CONTACTS

* I am pretty good friends with a girl in L.A. who lived with Courtney Love and Curt Cobain for
quite some time. I've been to the Hollywood Hills house where they once lived and where they
conceived their kid. Courtney love was hated by all her roomates.

This is important. Courtney Love is and was hated by nearly everybody who knew her.

* I am also acquainted with a girl here in Seattle who used to be C. Love's heroin-shooting pal
in San Francisco and she may have good stories.

* There is an audio tape I can get of both Cobain and Courtney (but mostly Courtney) repeatedly
calling up a woman named Virginia and threatening to kill her. Virgina is English and was
writing book that concerned either Cobain or Nirvana and I guess the two were scared she was
going to write something they didn't like.

Cobain says something like "I could hire a hit man for a couple thousand dollars but I'm going
to kill you myself. That's right I don't care if this is recorded -- I'm threatening to kill
you."

Melissa Rossi also has this tape but it's not generally in circulation.

* Another friend of mine's girlfriend works at Sub Pop record Co. (which produced(?) Nirvana)
her name is Nicky. According to Nicky (said my friend), the cops had been out to the house
where Cobain killed himself "several times" within the last month. That's all I could get out
of him and apparantly nobody is talking anymore. She had also told him not to say anything,
including what he told me. She's probably clammed up by now.

* Cobain had a massuese and a psychic (both women) who told a story of a tussle they were
involved in at Kurt's house (different house) in spring last year. It erupted after the psychic

read their auras and the massuse massaged them and Cobain resisted some sort of "cleansing
ritual" and got a gun and waved it around.

Maybe I could get to the massuse and/or the psychic thru a mutual friend. I don't know how
recently they may have seen Cobain. The massuese is named Elizabeth Finan and the Psychic's
first name is Laura.

Once again, all the people who would know anything have shut up for whatever reasons.

AT THE HOUSE

Kurt Cobain's house is at 171 Lake Washington Blvd. in the Seattle neighborhood of Madrona. His

house is right next to a small park and looks over Lake Washington toward Bill Gate's new compound under construction. Nice place.

Although newspapers have called it a "greenhouse" it seems he killed himself in the top of an
A-frame building, which was used as a spare room. There is a wooden deck and a sliding glass
door to the back. The bottom part is a garage. The upper part has long, tall windows, which are

more like skylights than anything else. By the time I arrived (about 5 pm) the body had been
removed and the place had been secured by private guards who wore no uniforms but did have fancy

headphone/microphone sets. Their hats said "Contemporary Services Corp. " Never heard of them.
They were polite but would not answer any questions or let anyone on the property.

While I was there Courtney Love showed up (perhaps around seven) in a limo with her baby and was

reportedly wearing a black jacket and had her hair in a pony tail. The limo left. By this
time, police had replaced private cops in securing the perimeter. A couple of people said they
saw her place the baby in one of the windows of the house. Possibly she did that on purpose?
To show people the kid?

A friend of mine shot several photos of the place, including a strange broken area in the fence
behind the house. It didn't seem to be freshly broken, but a gate was knocked in and opened
onto a stone path that led down to the A-frame below. I'm sure his pix are available if you
like.

Some neighborhood kids came by and said they didn't remember the gate being knocked down like
that but couldn't say for sure.

Most of the media whether local or out-of-town, seemed clueless. A guy named Bernard Gonzalez
(sp?) who I think is from Current Affair or some other Fox show was there doing feeds for news
shows (apparently). In between broadcasts he bitched that Cobain's suicide had made him miss
his kids' softball game and that now the kids would grow up to hate Nirvana. He also said he
had never heard of Nirvana before this morning.

Here are the license plate numbers and descriptions of some cars that were parked well inside
the property and may well have been there at the time Cobain killed himself.

Parked right next to the garage/A-frame was a 1964, '65 Valiant with two flat tires. Couldn't
see the plate.

There was also a Honda Accord plate No. 627 BQG (Wash. State).

A Subaru, license No. MAN 6G (WA)

A chrysler, plate no. IB4 CRY (WA)

One of the security cars was a Honda plate no. 472 CPD.

There are some strange things about this story. The newspaper accounts don't jibe with the
reality. I don't believe the letter was only one page long. I had the impression it was "quite

lengthy". Also the newspaper made the shotgun wound to the temple (they say) sound clean. I
had the impression earlier in the day that his head had nearly been blown off. In any case the
paper says the identification was done by fingerprints.

There's something to the mother angle. I think his mother was harassing him in some way. She
apparently called the cops to look for him when he left some kind of a "treatment center" and
the cops instructed "workers" at the house to call them if they saw Cobain. I don't see how it
would be possible to miss his presence. The place is not that big. The TV was on in the house.

The cops were never called even though there must have been signs of life there.

Anyway, everybody's shut up now and I don't know where the body is. There is *some* chance I
can find out and even get to it, especially if it's to be cremated.

Selected Bibliography

Books

Allen, Robert J., ed., *Addison and Steele: Selections from the "Tattler" and the "Spectator*," 2nd ed., Holt, Rinehart and Winston, 1970

Betrock, Alan, *Unseen Culture: The Roots of Cult*, Shake Books, 1994

Bird, S. Elizabeth, *For Enquiring Minds: A Cultural Study of Supermarket Tabloids*, University of Tennessee Press, 1992

Cross, Robert, "All News Is Good News for *Enquirer*," in *Stalking the Feature Story*, Ruehlmann, William, ed., Writer's Digest, 1977

Dannen, Frederic, *Hit Men: Power Brokers and Fast Money Inside the Music Business*, Times Books, 1990

Ethics Center Seminar of St. Petersburg, FL, *Making Sense of the News, Seminar at the Modern Media Institute*, 1983

Halperin, Morton, et al., *The Lawless State: The Crimes of the U.S. Intelligence Agencies*, Penguin, 1976

Hougan, Jim, *Secret Agenda: Watergate, Deep Throat, and the CIA*, Random House, 1983

Lacey, Robert, *Little Man: Meyer Lansky and the Gangster Life*, Little, Brown, 1991

Maas, Peter, *The Valachi Papers*, Bantam Books, 1972

Marchetti, Victor, and John D. Marks, *The CIA and the Cult of Intelligence*, Knopf, 1974

Mayer, Martin, *Making News*, Harvard Business School Press, 1993

Morrow, Robert D., *The Senator Must Die*, Roundtable, 1988

Piper, Michael Collins, *Final Judgment*, Wolfe Press, 1993

Pritchard, Peter, *The Making of McPaper: The Inside Story of "USA Today*," Gannett News Media Services, 1987

Taylor, S. J., *Shock! Horror! The Tabloids in Action*, Bantam Press, 1991

Von Hoffman, Nicholas, *Citizen Cohn: The Life and Times of Roy Cohn*, Doubleday, 1988

Wolf, George, and Joseph DiMona, *Frank Costello: Prime Minister of the Underworld*, William Morrow, 1974

Journal and Newspaper Articles

"Amazing and All True! Lawyers Reveal Secrets for Protecting Tabs," *New York Times*, 4 Jan. 1991

Associated Press, "*Enquirer* Charged on Alien Laws," *New York Times*, 21 Nov. 1981

Associated Press, "Infuriated Minds Battling *Enquirer*: Lawsuits Take Aim at Tabloid," *The Montreal Gazette*, 16 Oct. 1990

Auletta, Ken, "The Fall of Lehman Brothers: The Men, the Money, the Merger," pt. 2, *New York Times*, 24 Feb. 1985

Bagdikian, Ben, "Conquering Hearts and Minds: The Lords of the Global Village," *The Nation*, vol. 248, no. 23, 2 June 1989

"Barr Produces More Ammo for Lawsuit Against Tabloid," *People*, 10 Jan. 1991

Beyette, Beverly, "Celebrities Are Out to Beat Tabloids at Their Own Game," *Los Angeles Times*, 29 Sept. 1989

Brownstein, Bill, "Nobody Likes Supermarket Tabloids—Except 14 Million Readers," *The Montreal Gazette*, 12 Jan. 1991

Burton, Michael, "U.S. Media Look Back at Desert Storm: The Iraqis that 'Got Away,' " *Extra!* Apr./May 1992

Clausen, Christopher, "Reading the Supermarket Tabloids," *The New Leader*, 7 Sept. 1992

Frankel, Glenn, "Media Baron Sues Seymour Hersh: Robert Maxwell Denies Author's Charge of Aiding Israeli Spies, *Washington Post*, 25 Oct. 1991

Gitlin, Todd, "Media Lemmings Run Amok!" *Washington Journalism Review*, Apr. 1992

Gladwell, Malcolm, "From Paper to Reader, Something Gets Inferred in the Translation," *Washington Post*, 16 March 1992

Guy, Pat, "Alien Tabloids Plan to Merge! OK, Not Quite," *USA Today*, 30 March 1990

"Hollywood Goes to War," *Time*, 21 Jan. 1980

Hubbell, Sue, "Rare Glimpse Inside Tabloid World Reveals Editor Is a Mad Dog! *Smithsonian*, Oct. 1993

"It's Star Wars on the Tabs," *People*, 15 Oct. 1990

James, Meg, "Court Rules Media Can Name Rape Victims," *Palm Beach Post*, 9 Dec. 1994

Kelm, Rebecca Sturm, "The Lack of Access to Back Issues of the Weekly Tabloids: Does It Matter?" *The Centennial Review*, vol. 34, no. 2, spring 1990

Kirchheimer, Sid, "Enquiring Minds Want to Know the Man Behind the *National Enquirer*," *Fort Lauderdale News & Sun-Sentinel*, 25 Feb. 1987

Lutton, Wayne, "Book Review: *Cults That Kill: Probing the Underworld of Occult Crime* by Larry Kahaner," *National Review*, vol. 40, no. 21, 28 Oct. 1988

Marbin, Carol, "Ex-cult Hero Sues Tabloid; Ed Anger Is 'Pig-Biting' Mad," *Palm Beach Post*, 14 Oct. 1989

"Marla Maples' Mother Sues *National Enquirer*," *Washington Times*, 6 July 1990

McDowell, Edwin, "Time Out for Writers' Conferences," *New York Times*, 27 May 1983

Meyers, Bobbie, "Stakeout Secrets Revealed," *Palm Beach Post*, 13 June 1987

"Murphy Dismisses Pope Jr. as Honorary Police Deputy," *New York Times*, 26 Oct. 1950

New York Times Service, "Tabloids' 'Scorpion Defence' Stings," *Globe & Mail*, 4 Jan. 1994

"Oprah Winfrey and Stedman Graham File $300 Million Suit Against Toronto-based Tabloid," *Jet*, vol. 81, no. 253, Apr. 1992

Peterson, Mark Allen, "Aliens, Ape Men and Whacky Savages: The Anthropologist in the Tabloids," *Anthropology Today*, vol. 7, no. 5, Oct. 1991

Playboy, "History of Organized Crime" series, 1973–1974

Randall, Michael H., "*National Enquirer*," *Whole Earth Review*, 22 Sept. 1986

Reilly, Patrick M., "Maxwell Nabs Three Supermarket Tabs," *Wall Street Journal*, 17 May 1990

Roach, Mary, "Tabloid Secrets Revealed!" *In Health*, vol. 4, no. 6, Nov., Dec. 1990

Schreiner, Tim, "You Can't Ignore News . . . and Those Tabs Aren't All from Mars Any Longer," *Washington Journalism Review*, Apr. 1992

Shiras, Ginger, "First Amendment, Taste *Sun* Defense," *Seattle Times*, 4 Dec. 1991

Shiras, Ginger, "Invasion of Privacy Costs $1.5 Million," *Seattle Times*, 5 Dec. 1991

Shiras, Ginger, "*Sun* Says Stories Fiction," *Seattle Times*, 3 Dec. 1991

Slack, Lyle, "Alien Brainchild Lands in Supermarket, Libels Oprah, Dies," *Saturday Night*, Nov. 1992

Smilgis, Martha, "In Florida: The Rogues of Tabloid Valley," *Time*, 15 Aug. 1988

Smith, Liz, "An Angry Steve McQueen Joins Anti-*Enquirer* Army," *Detroit Free Press*, 24 March 1980

"Sorry, Shirley (and Surely Sorry)," *Time*, 9 May 1984

"Suit Dismissed Against Liberace," *USA Today*, 6 Apr. 1987

Thomas, Evan, "Inherit the Mint: How Edward Bennett Williams Made Legal Prostitution Respectable," *Washington Monthly*, vol. 23, no. 10, Oct. 1991

"Thomas Sues *Enquirer*," *Sunday Sentinel*, 25 Dec. 1986

"*Time's* 25 Most Influential Americans: Steve Coz, Editor, *National Enquirer*," *Time*, 21 Apr. 1997

Tolpin, James H. "Former Musician, Newspaper Settle Libel Suit," *Fort Lauderdale News & Sun-Sentinel*, 19 Feb. 1987

Wilson, Mike, "Cat Stevens Settles Suit Against Tabloid," *Miami Herald*, 19 Feb. 1987

Prevailing Winds Magazine and Catalogue

The following articles come from *Prevailing Winds Research*, a publication of The Center for the Preservation of Modern History. They are either reprints or articles commissioned by the magazine. *Prevailing Winds*, PO Box 23511, Santa Barbara, CA 93121, (805) 899-3433; fax: (805) 899-4773

Agee, Phillip, "Producing the Proper Crisis: A Speech by Phillip Agee"

Anderson, Robin, "Propaganda and the Media"

Anson, Robert Sam, "The Smartest Spy"

Bagdikian, Ben, "The Media Silence"

Bokaer, Joan, "Fundamentalism and the New Right"

Chomsky, Noam, and Jeff Cohen, "The Manipulated Media"

"CIA Relations with Media—Official and Otherwise," collection of articles from *Covert Action Information Bulletin*, no. 7, Dec. 1979

Connolly, John, "Inside the Shadow CIA," *Spy*, Sept. 1992

Gelbspan, Ross, "The New FBI"

Herman, Edward S., "Disinformation as News Fit to Print"

Kohn, Howard, "The Nixon-Hughes-Lansky Connection," *Rolling Stone*, 1976

Lyon, Verne, "The History of Operation CHAOS"

Marchetti, Victor, "Twilight of the Spooks"

Pearson, David, "The Media and Government Deception"

Reed, Cyrus, "Two from the Tico Times"

Russell, Dick, "Non-Lethal Defense"

Schoenman, Ralph, "Iraq and Kuwait: A History Suppressed"

Sheehan, Daniel, "The Persian Gulf War, Covert Operations and the New World Order"

Schefflin, Allan W., and Edward M. Optin Jr., "The Quest for the Manchurian Candidate"

Sims, Rebecca, "The CIA and Financial Institutions"

Sinkin, Larry, "Waco, Koresh and Mind Control," *Portland Free Press*

Steiner, Ralph, "Sting/Counter-Sting: Unmasking the Disinformers"

Summers, Anthony, "Hidden Hoover," *Vanity Fair*, March 1993

"Transcript of the Meeting Between Saddam Hussein and U.S. Ambassador April Glaspie," 29 July 1990

Trento, Joe, and Dave Roman, "The Spies Who Came in from the Newsroom"

"Victor Marchetti: A *Penthouse* Interview"

Witanek, Robert, "Students, Scholars, and Spies: The CIA on Campus," *Covert Action Information Bulletin*, winter 1989

Other Sources

Lowell, Sandra, ed., *Tabloid Tattler*, PO Box 93944, Hollywood, CA 90093-0944

Popular Culture Library, Bowling Green State University, Bowling Green, OH 43403-0600, (419) 372-2450

Skeptical Enquirer, published by the Committee for the Scientific Investigation of Claims of the Paranormal

Sleazy Business: A Pictorial History of Exploitation Tabloids, 1959–1974; Unseen America: The Greatest Cult Exploitation Magazines, 1950–1966—available through Shake Books, 449 12th St., Brooklyn, NY 11215, (718) 499-6941

Transcript of *"National Enquirer," 60 Minutes*, vol. VIII, no. 13, CBS, 7 March 1976, Harry Moses, producer

New from Feral House

VIRTUAL GOVERNMENT
CIA MIND CONTROL OPERATIONS IN AMERICA
Alex Constantine

Further remarkable revelations from the author of *Psychic Dictatorship in the USA*. *Virtual Government* includes a chapter on the mobster and drug connection to the murder of Nicole Simpson, information that will be used in an upcoming documentary on the infamous crime. "Alex Constantine is the foremost journalist and contemporary historian of the murky worlds of vice and vice-squads."—Donald Freed.
PAPERBACK • 6 X 9 • $14.95

KILLER FICTION
G. J. Schaefer, as Told to Sondra London
Introduction by Colin Wilson

These vile, fetishistic stories were used in court to convict Schaefer of serial murder. Schaefer, recently stabbed to death in prison, received his literary training from novelist Harry Crews, and researched his books practicing the sordid crimes detailed within. Includes illustrations. Adults Only!
PAPERBACK • 6 X 9 • $14.95

THE OCTOPUS
SECRET GOVERNMENT & THE DEATH OF DANNY CASOLARO
Kenn Thomas and Jim Keith

This extraordinary book uses the actual notes of Danny Casolaro, a journalist murdered investigating a nexus of crime he called "The Octopus," since it led a torturous course from software manufacturers to Hollywood to Indian Reservations to the Department of Justice.
HARDCOVER • 6 X 9 • $19.95

The titles above may be ordered from Feral House for check or money order plus $2 each book ordered for shipping. For a free catalogue of publications, send an SASE.

Feral House • 2532 Lincoln Blvd., Suite 359 • Venice, CA • 90291